Fischli and Weiss

The Way Things Go

Jeremy Millar

One Work Series Editor
Mark Lewis

Afterall Books Editors
Charles Esche and Mark Lewis

Managing Editor
Caroline Woodley

Picture Research
Gaia Alessi

Copy Editor
Tavia Fortt

Other titles in the *One Work* series:

Bas Jan Ader: In Search of the Miraculous
by Jan Verwoert

Hollis Frampton: (nostalgia)
by Rachel Moore

Ilya Kabakov: The Man Who Flew into Space from his Apartment
by Boris Groys

Richard Prince: Untitled (couple)
by Michael Newman

Joan Jonas: I Want to Live in the Country (And Other Romances)
by Susan Morgan

Mary Heilmann: Save the Last Dance for Me
by Terry R. Myers

Marc Camille Chaimowicz: Celebration? Realife
by Tom Holert

Yvonne Rainer: The Mind is a Muscle
by Catherine Wood

One Work is a unique series of books published by Afterall, based at Central Saint Martins College of Art and Design in London. Each book presents a single work of art considered in detail by a single author. The focus of the series is on contemporary art and its aim is to provoke debate about significant moments in art's recent development.

Over the course of more than 100 books, important works will be presented in a meticulous and generous manner by writers who believe passionately in the originality and significance of the works about which they have chosen to write. Each book contains a comprehensive and detailed formal description of the work, followed by a critical mapping of the aesthetic and cultural context in which it was made and has gone on to shape. The changing presentation and reception of the work throughout its existence is also discussed and each writer stakes a claim on the influence 'their' work has on the making and understanding of other works of art.

The books insist that a single contemporary work of art (in all of its different manifestations) can, through a unique and radical aesthetic articulation or invention, affect our understanding of art in general. More than that, these books suggest that a single work of art can literally transform, however modestly, the way we look at and understand the world. In this sense the *One Work* series, while by no means exhaustive, will eventually become a veritable library of works of art that have made a difference.

First published in 2007
by Afterall Books

Afterall
Central Saint Martins
College of Art and Design
University of the Arts London
107–109 Charing Cross Road
London WC2H ODU
www.afterall.org

ISBN Paperback: 978-1-84638-035-8
ISBN Cloth: 978-1-84638-036-5

Distribution by The MIT Press, Cambridge,
Massachusetts and London
www.mitpress.mit.edu

Art Direction and Typeface Design
A2/SW/HK

Printed and bound by
Die Keure, Belgium

Fischli and Weiss images courtesy the artists,
Monika Sprüth Philomene Magers, Cologne/
Munich/London, Galerie Eva Presenhuber, Zürich
and Matthew Marks Gallery, New York.

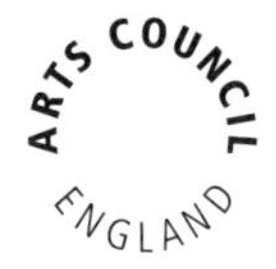

Fischli and Weiss
The Way Things Go

Jeremy Millar

With sincere thanks to Lilian Haberer at Monika Sprüth Philomene Magers for her attempts to obtain answers to my many questions; Michael Newhall for his references on humour and to Ceal Floyer for the great joke; Mark Godfrey for his notes on the artists; Hans Ulrich Obrist for his time; Brian Dillon for the great number of conversations on subjects related to this essay; the late Tony Wilson for introducing this film to me and to Russell Haswell for coming to the ICA that first time to see it.

Most of all, I would like to thank Karen Eslea and Florence Millar for their patience, understanding and love, which have made this, and all else, possible. This book is dedicated to them.

The author and editors would also like to thank Pablo Lafuente at Afterall, Thomas Jarek and Markus Rischgasser at Eva Presenhuber and Mrs. J.C. Robinson at the estate of William Heath Robinson.

Jeremy Millar is an artist and AHRC Research Fellow in the Creative and Performing Arts, Ruskin School of Drawing and Fine Art, University of Oxford.

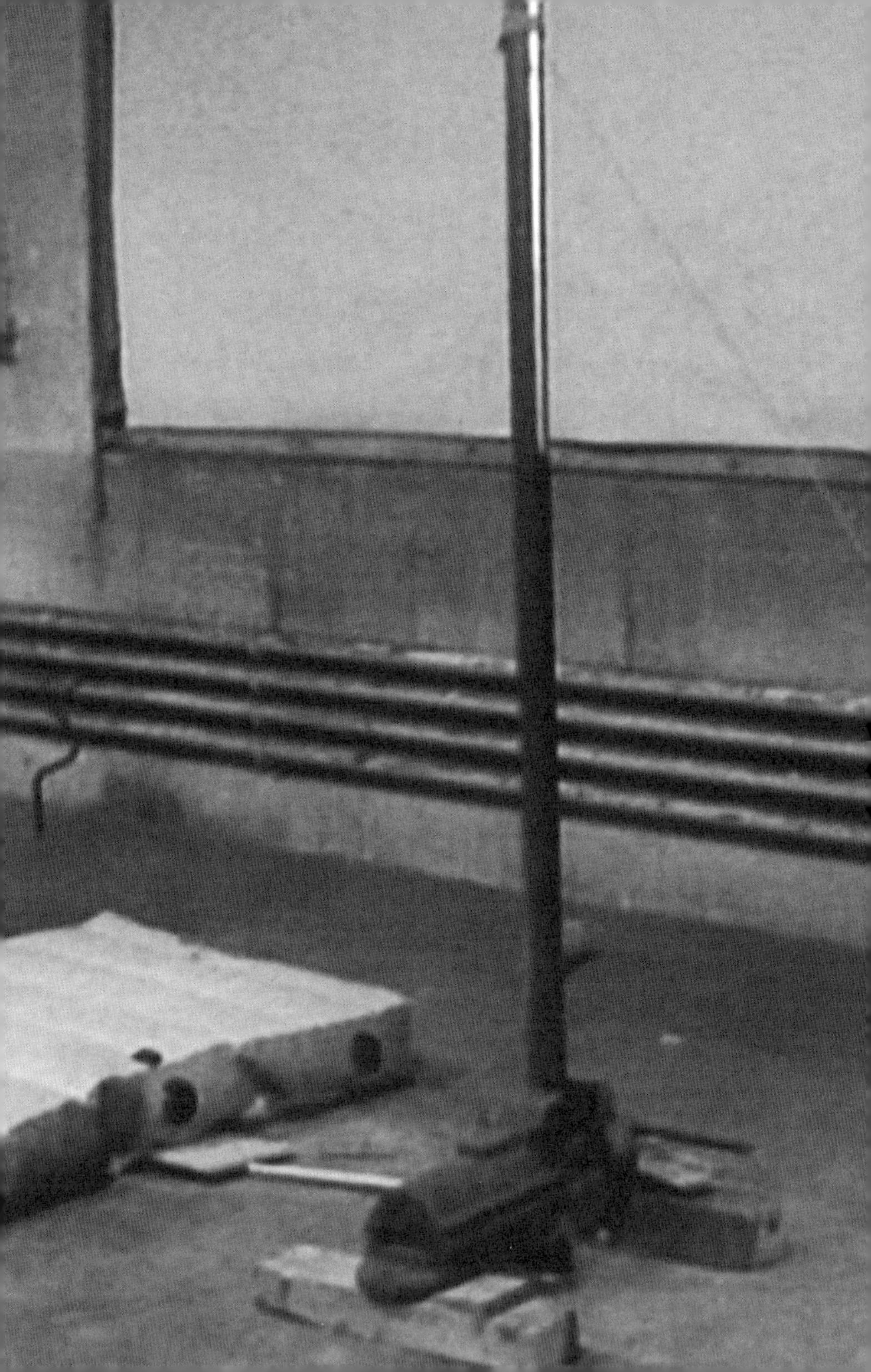

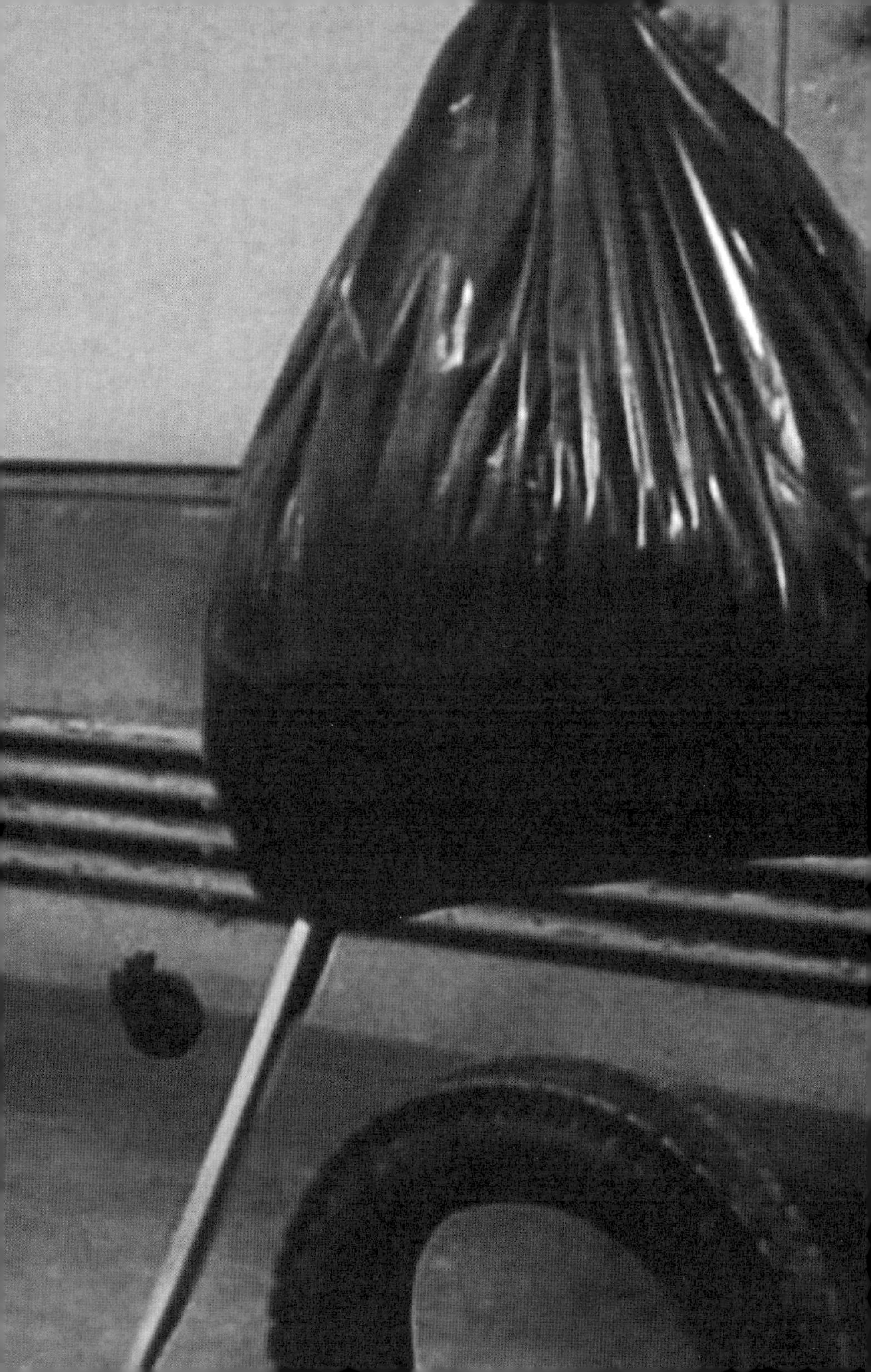

previous page

Still from *The Way Things Go*,
16mm colour film, 30mins, 1987.

We react to the cause. Calling something 'the cause' is like pointing and saying, 'He's to blame!'
— Ludwig Wittgenstein

I cannot now remember which sequence within Peter Fischli and David Weiss's extraordinary film *Der Lauf der Dinge* (*The Way Things Go*, 1987) I saw first, but I do remember when and where I saw it. It was in the early hours of the morning one weekday in 1988, and I was in the family living room watching 'The Other Side of Midnight', an arts-magazine programme created and presented by Tony Wilson, Granada TV newsreader, co-founder of Factory Records and Manchester legend. As I remember it, the programme was coming to an end when Wilson announced that he was about to show a clip from a wonderful film by two Swiss artists that was then showing at the ICA in London; the film was *so* good, Wilson insisted, that everyone should go to London to see it. It was this that really made me take note. For Wilson, as militantly Mancunian as he was, to suggest a trip to London for *anything* — now this really was something, and therefore suggested that the film must really be something else.[1] Of course, even from that short extract on late-night television, even through bleary teenage eyes, it was obvious to me that this film really *was* something, a seemingly chaotic, obviously choreographed sequence of everyday objects crashing, falling, tipping, rolling, one into, onto, over another, and this then, in turn, taking its turn in the seemingly never-ending sequence of controlled catastrophe. It was also laugh-out-loud funny. The following morning at school, I spoke with my friend Russell, who'd also watched the programme, and we decided then that we must take the train to London as soon as we could.

This was the first time that either of us had visited the ICA, although in time the gallery would become familiar to both of us. It took a little while to find the film, which was being projected in one of the ornate Nash rooms upstairs, but its clatter cascaded down and we strained necks around the heavy wooden door and slipped into the darkness and onto empty seats at the back. Of course it was already underway, the balloons filling or falling, chairs tipping, trolleys slipping down slopes or fired by fireworks, tyres tripping along a ladder's rungs and then the great pile-up toward the end, a whole stack tilting like a building in an earth-quake, the oblong space beneath a table becoming now a parallelogram, and increasingly narrow, nudging then collapsing, falling heavy and unfeeling until a bucket tips water onto a pile of solid dry ice and its vapour spills like apocalyptic waves across the bare concrete floor. And as the film faded to black and the credits began to roll up the screen, the audience — perhaps only another half-dozen people — stood up and began to clap, and continued to clap until the credits came to an end. Unfamiliar with gallery etiquette, we of course did the same, assuming that this was what happened in art galleries, and how one responded to contemporary artists' films. I've seen a few more since then, but this is still the only time I witnessed an audience standing and applauding the greatness of the work, not simply the presence of the artist.

We stayed and watched it again, in its entirety, and laughed and snorted amazement once more, and could have continued to do so all afternoon. Even in our ignorance, and mine more than Russell's, it was clear that we had watched something great. For perhaps the very first time, art, and in particular a work of contemporary art, seemed important enough to become my future. It was a little frightening, being moved like this — moved but not touched, like the empty cardboard box near the end that is fanned forward by a falling wooden board — uncertain what would come next, or what might have to.

Of course, ours was not the first delight to be had in front of Fischli and Weiss's film. It was first shown the previous year, when it was included in the 1987 iteration of Documenta, the major international exhibition of contemporary art held every five years in the German town of Kassel, where it became a massive popular success. Since then, it has been included in countless group exhibitions and screenings, and shown in its entirety on television (under the title *Chain Reaction*); unusually for an artists' film, it even became available to buy on VHS, and more recently on DVD, in gallery shops and art bookstores. I have heard kids, themselves fragile and combustible, ignite with enthusiasm in describing it, as have professors for whom this was clearly not their first experience of art (although it seemed to feel so). The philosopher Arthur C. Danto, in his brilliance, writes essays on it; my four-year-old daughter, in her brilliance, asks to watch it on TV. It is a work — and this is a rare thing indeed

— about which I have yet to hear a bad word spoken, a work whose public popularity has not diminished the seriousness with which it is regarded by people within the 'art world'. Of course, it is not uncommon for 'professionals' to dislike art which is popular, although more often than not this is because the work is bad, rather than the fact of its popularity. What makes it bad can often be what can make it popular; with *The Way Things Go*, on the other hand, what makes it popular also makes it good. The work has been 'borrowed' for advertisements (for cars, phone services and radio football commentary) and for pop videos, and now people have begun posting their own table-top attempts on YouTube. Twenty years after it was first exhibited, *The Way Things Go* is perhaps as popular as it has ever been.

Of course, it is difficult enough to write on artworks, let alone on one so well-known and so well-loved. To write about why it is so good, about why it is so funny, seems a thankless task; there can be few things as bad, or as unfunny, one would think. In considering this work in greater detail, however, I shall do more than reconsider general assumptions about the film. I shall consider *The Way Things Go* in relation not only to some of Fischli and Weiss's other works, but also to some artists, writers and their works from the past. I will also consider in some detail notions of mechanisation, boredom, humour and wonder, drawing from a broad range of thinkers and writers. In so doing, I hope to gain a better understanding of what it is that makes this film so important, and in turn a more general sense of what is so important in the making of, and thinking about, art more generally. If at times this seems a little digressive, then this is in keeping with the subject at hand, and I feel able to agree with Laurence Sterne (with whom the artists must surely empathise) when he writes in *Tristram Shandy* (1759) that 'Digressions, incontestably, are the sunshine — they are the life, the soul of reading — take them out of this book for instance — you might as well take the book along with them.'[2]

It is possible to discern numerous historic influences within *The Way Things Go*, some of which I shall turn to in due course; however, the most immediate precedent is another work by Fischli and Weiss, the series of relatively small colour and black-and-white photographs known as *Stiller Nachmittag* (*Quiet Afternoon*), or alternatively *Equilibres*, from 1984–86. In each of these photographs, one finds a number of different objects — sometimes as few as three, sometimes more than 20 — that have been placed in a precarious balance, or a 'provisional arrangement', to quote the title of one such work. The objects used are everyday items found within the kitchen, or the artists' studio — carrots, graters, wine bottles, chairs and assorted cutlery from the former; ladders, tyres, saws, aerosol cans and buckets from the latter — which have been coaxed into an extraordinary array of assemblages and then photographed, one suspects, just prior to their collapsing in an unceremonious heap on table-top or floor. And so, as if petrified in the cold light of the camera's flash or a photo-lamp, a chair is wedged impassibly with buckets and a tyre in a door-frame; a courgette sits hunched upon a carrot held horizontally in the handle of a grater; and an empty wine bottle sits upon a saw whose elegantly curved blade is snagged in a length of see-sawed wood.

But how might one consider these works? I want to begin with the photograph opposite. On the left, a torn scrap of orange foam sits upon a slanted strip of wood, a smoking cigarette at its end, the wood lying across the cut, upturned base of a plastic bottle (that was previously used to store paintbrushes, it would seem) which, in turn, is angled upon the shaft of a hammer, the metal head now acting like a pair of splayed feet. In the middle, a russet pear has been placed upside down in the neck of a cardboard tube, a bottle-top for its crown, while rusted metal tubing sweeps down, a strip of wire hooked at its end, across which is stretched a paint-stained yellow rubber glove. To the right, the metal tube rests on the toe of a dusty blue plimsoll that stands back on its heel, another lit cigarette here held nonchalantly in its laces, as if on a bottom lip.

Perhaps one might consider the formal aspects more seriously, beyond the helpless anthropomorphisms already described, noting the 'three discrete figures combined to yield one unified entity'; indeed, one might go further to applaud the 'supreme crystalline repose in the composition as a whole and – in starkest contrast – the most vigorous movement in the three figures individually'. But this would be, instead, to quote

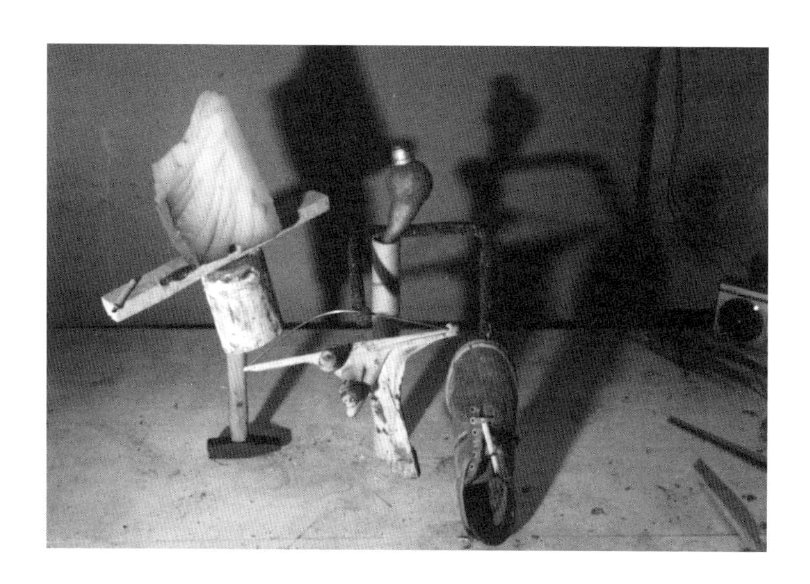

Mrs. Pear bringing her husband
a freshly ironed shirt for the opera.
The boy smokes., photograph,
1984–86.

Aloïs Riegl's description of *Laocoön and His Sons*, the great Hellenistic marble that now resides in the Vatican, and whatever formal similarities the two works might share —which, admittedly, might not be immediately apparent — such visual scrutiny, however acute, seems misplaced here.[3] Our traditional means of formal analysis seem unable to deal with works, such as these, that are less concerned with external appearance than with 'internal' conceptual coherence. Indeed, when one learns the title of this strange photograph — *Mrs. Pear bringing her husband a freshly ironed shirt for the opera. The boy smokes.* — then the separation between this work and the Vatican marble widens further; the serpentine agonies of the Trojan seer and his sons in 'a work to be preferred to all that the arts of painting and sculpture have produced' have been replaced by the haphazard approximation of petit bourgeois domesticity.[4] 'A deadly fraud is this', might be overstating it, but there remains quite a distinction nonetheless.[5]

Fanged humour aside, it is clear that the compositional arrangement arrived at by Fischli and Weiss here, and indeed in the other photographs in the series, is subject to markedly different forces than those that might be found in more classically constructed works. The materials pictured are lowly, and their forms often mangled or distressed; the arrangements in which they are placed seem awkward, and colour, when it appears, does so apologetically and with a shrug. But these are all aspects that can be seen, that are perceptible to the viewer, and one is right to suspect that there are greater hidden forces at work here — most obviously and notably that of gravity. These are pictures of something invisible, and as one looks through these works, one senses that the artist's hand can intuit that which escapes the viewer's eye. These are pictures created in deference to an inescapable force, albeit not some transcendental entity that might attempt to elevate the form, but rather a force that drags indiscriminately upon its very materiality. One must not necessarily consider this a burden, however; on the contrary, finding oneself relieved of such a mystical 'spirit', or even a notion of good taste, can have a liberating effect. As Fischli has remarked, 'In the *Equilibres* we were slightly relieved of the question of which object must be selected according to which criteria: it doesn't matter whether the colour of the cigarette lighter that establishes and maintains the balance is a nice green or not [...] if it stays up, then it can only be good.'[6]

On occasion, as in the case of *Mrs. Pear bringing her husband a freshly ironed shirt for the opera. The boy smokes.*, an implicit narrative might be found in some of these works. If it is, however, it tends to be supplementary to the fundamental arrangement of the objects, and one suspects it has only been identified and developed as the placement is coming, or indeed already has come, to an end. Most especially, it is the title itself, which of course resides outside the image, that can prod the story forward, and in so doing throw our own expectations off-balance with no fear of toppling the rather precarious objects themselves. This rather unusual sense of narrative construction — an external mechanism that shapes the forms within these photographs, working invisibly but undeniably upon their very matter — is in some sense reminiscent of the *procédé* of the extraordinary French writer Raymond Roussel, and I think it would be well worth exploring his writing further in order to better understand the particular nature of Fischli and Weiss's own procedure. As far as I am aware, Fischli and Weiss have never acknowledged Roussel as an influence on their practice, but there are qualities in their sculptures that brings to mind the invention of Roussel's novels, and one might discern interesting similarities between the works of the writer and those of the artists, including *The Way Things Go*.

Born in 1877 to an extraordinarily wealthy family that belonged to the Parisian *haute bourgeoisie*, Roussel was a near-neighbour of the Prousts, who lived further down Boulevard Malesherbes. In his notebook, Michel Leiris, a long-time friend whose father was Roussel's financial advisor, pondered the similarities between the two writers:

They were from the same epoch, and both were rich, bourgeois and homosexual. Both shared the same taste for 'imitation'. The same way of looking at things as if through a microscope. The same cult of childhood memories. Haunted by the passing of time and by death. Sought refuge, not in God, but in a universe unique to each, but which was created from all sorts of bits and pieces. Both escaped into vaudeville, into trivial, even scatological humour. [...] *Same absence of conformism under 'orthodox' exteriors.*[7]

Excepting the more personal details, one might recognise much of this — fascination with imitation, and with childhood; salvation in the remnants of everyday life; humour; disguised non-conformity — in the work of Fischli and Weiss as well.

Despite the relative obscurity of his writings — that is, both their inherent 'difficulty' and the general lack of interest in them — Roussel can quite easily be claimed as one of the most influential writers of the twentieth century, if only for his acknowledged importance to undoubtedly the most influential artist of that century, Marcel Duchamp. 'It was fundamentally Roussel who was responsible for my "Glass", *La mariée mise à nu par ses célibataires, même* (*The Bride Stripped Bare by Her Bachelors, Even*, 1915–23)', he commented in an interview in 1946. 'From his *Impressions d'Afrique* I got the general approach [...] Roussel showed me the way.' Later, in 1963, Roussel was claimed in an essay as a precursor by Alain Robbe-Grillet, the primary writer and theorist of the *nouveau roman*, while in that same year, Michel Foucault published his only book of literary criticism, which was devoted to Roussel.[8]

The most important and influential book of Roussel's, however, was the one written about his own works. Published in 1935, two years after his suicide in a Palermo hotel, *Comment j'ai écrit certains de mes livres* (*How I Wrote Certain of My Books*) sets out the various methods and procedures by which Roussel created the extraordinary scenes to be found in works such as the novels *Impressions d'Afrique* (*Impressions of Africa*, 1910) and *Locus Solus*, 1914), and the incredible complexity of his poem *Nouvelles Impressions d'Afrique* (*New Impressions of Africa*, 1932). As with Fischli and Weiss, a rigorous play is fundamental to Roussel's practice. He provides a famous example of his *procédé* from the story *Parmi les Noirs* (*Among the Blacks*, 1935), written when he was in his early twenties. Like other stories of his written at around the same time, *Parmi les Noirs* begins and ends with phrases that are identical except for a single letter; however, each main word has a different meaning from its mirror image at the other end of the work. So, the story begins with '*Les letters du blanc sur les bandes du vieux billard*' (The letters [of the alphabet] in white [chalk] on the cushions of the old billiard table), and finishes with '*les lettres du blanc sur les bandes du vieux pillard*' (the letters [correspondence] sent by the white man about the hordes of the old plunderer). As Roussel remarked, once he had found these two phrases, it was then simply a question of writing the narrative that would bring them together.

Although Roussel's method for writing or constructing the text was a little different in *Impressions d'Afrique* – 'I chose a word and then linked it to another by the preposition *à* [with]; and these two words, each capable of more than one meaning, supplied me with a further creation' – it produced similarly extraordinary results.[9] In one memorable scene, minute pictures are produced within the flesh of ten white grapes, each of them ripened within a matter of seconds by means of a curious device utilising a 'dazzling beam of light' and a 'heavily compressed gas'. The mechanism appears somewhat *ad hoc*, like those to be found within *The Way Things Go*. The descriptions of the pictures also share something with the work of Fischli and Weiss. Their sculptural assemblages may not share the 'delicacy of the lines' or the 'luminous effulgence' of these curious examples of viniculture, but works such as *Ben Hur* from the series *Equilibres*, or *St Francis preaches to the animals on the purity of the heart* and *Herr and Frau Einstein shortly after the conception of their son, the genius Albert* from *Suddenly This Overview* (1981) are brought to mind when one reads of a grape which shows 'the circus in Rome, packed with a large crowd, watching with excitement a fight between gladiators'; of 'three grapes which hung side by side from the same parent stalk', each showing a scene 'from the Gospel of St. Luke'; or 'the first pangs of love, experienced by Jean-Jacques Rousseau's *Émile*'.[10] This is not to say that Fischli and Weiss's works were developed out of the marvellous creations within *Impressions d'Afrique*, whether consciously or otherwise, but rather to observe that all of these works share an incongruity of tone, and that they invite us to respond seriously and with sensitivity regardless of the absurdity of the situation in which we might find them, or ourselves.[11]

For Roussel, the procedures were 'essentially a poetic method' analogous to that of rhyme, a form of constraint that forces the writer to devise otherwise unforeseen combinations; I would suggest that, for Fischli and Weiss, the force of gravity on their everyday objects had

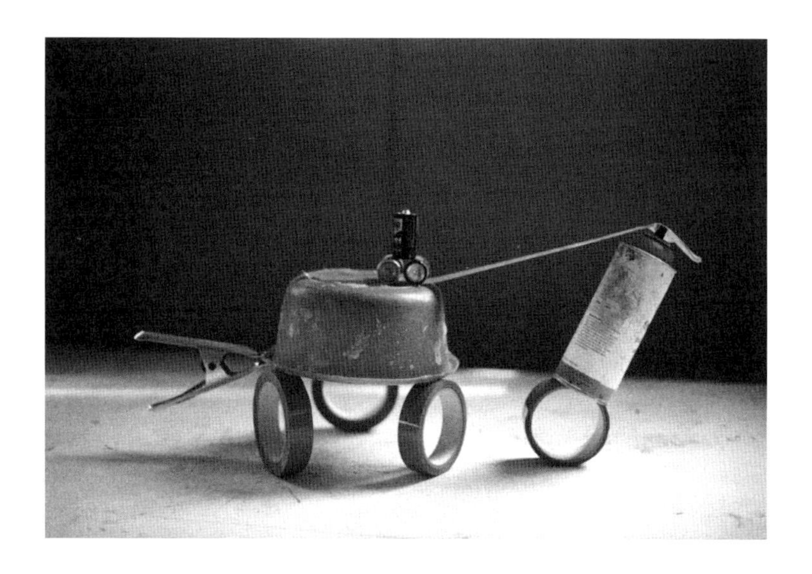

Ben Hur, photograph, 1984–86.

a similar effect. Both procedures are mere compositional techniques, and can in no way assure a work of any value. Roussel was clear: 'Just as one can use rhymes to compose good or bad verses, so one can use this method to produce good or bad works.'[12] As Roussel himself declined to present the *procédé* as a form of justification for the aesthetic value work, Fischli has spoken of *Equilibres* similarly: 'There was apparently no way to do it "better" or "worse", just "correctly".'[13]

The Danish philosopher Søren Kierkegaard once remarked that 'Boredom is the root of all evil', and while it would undoubtedly be unfair to judge the work of Fischli and Weiss so harshly, it is certainly true that its relationship to the tedious is an important one.[14] At times it may be the viewer that feels this numbed state of mind most keenly (or should that be most dully?), or who anticipates its onset — one might think of approaching the 12 monitors and 96 hours of video that constitute *Untitled* (1995), or of the anonymous modernity of *Settlements, Agglomerations* (1993) or even of what might be considered the banal spectacle of *Visible World* (1987—2001). At other times, one senses that it is the artists themselves who have succumbed, and as the son of a Protestant pastor, David Weiss is no doubt well aware that the devil makes work for idle hands. (However, with the possible exception of parts of *Fever*, 1983—84, *Fotografías*, 2004—05, and *An Unsettled Work*, 2000—06, there is little that one might consider diabolical in these artists' work.)

Concerns over the connection between boredom and bad behaviour are nothing new, regardless of how familiar we are with it being used within contemporary society either to understand or to excuse certain actions. The Early Christian Fathers considered their own notion of boredom, *acedia* — a Latin word, from the Greek *akedia* meaning 'absence of caring' — to be the gravest of the sins, for all the others were derived from it. It is interesting that one of the most important of these 'Desert Fathers', St. John Cassian, whose spiritual traditions have influenced a wide range of thinkers from St. Benedict to Michel Foucault, was even able to identify the period when this torpor was most likely to strike the solitary monk or desert hermit, referring to it as the *daemon meridianus*, the midday demon. Perhaps they rise a little later than these early mystics, but the arrival of Fischli and Weiss's own acedic demon is a little delayed, appearing at their studio retreat during the 'quiet afternoon'. St. John Cassian's remedy for this feeling of inertness was sustained physical activity, a tradition of the desert hermits, and indeed St. Paul the Hermit regularly wove baskets of palm leaves. However, while his isolation necessitated that he burned what he produced once a year, the results of Fischli and Weiss's own diverting activities were far less enduring, and destroyed themselves almost as soon as they were made, persisting now only as photographic records. If Nietzsche considered boredom 'the unpleasant "calm" of the soul' that preceded creative acts, then perhaps one might consider *Equilibres* the necessary preparation for the extraordinary compendium of activity that is *The Way Things Go*.

Whether constructed of masonry, carved in marble, cast in bronze, fixed beneath varnish, engraved on copper or on wood, a work of art is motionless only in appearance. It seems to be set fast – arrested, as are the moments of time gone by. But in reality it is born of change, and it leads to other changes.[15]

For the French art historian Henri Focillon, art was always dynamic, always shifting, riven by fractures and discontinuities, unstable and off-balance. As the title of his most famous book, *The Life of Forms in Art* (1934), makes clear, form is never static, however fixed it might seem at first glance, or even second, or much later still; form is alive, vital and always mobile. The forms within art – even within the plastic arts of sculpture or photography, as opposed to those that are more obviously performative – are 'subjected to the principle of metamorphoses, by which they are perpetually renewed', a process that is always already underway during the development of the forms themselves, and that continues even when they appear to be at rest. That form 'suggests to us the existence of other forms' seems undeniable when one considers the works within *Equilibres*, or looks through the artists' book produced to accompany the exhibition of these photographs at Ileana Sonnabend's New York gallery in 1986. *Provisional Arrangement*, for example, takes the elevated dining chair of The Confessional and sits upon it a mobile of small objects; *Chinese Symbol* takes the bent wire and wooden-handled brush of *The Pause*, removes the small cup and cigarette on which both ends of the wire were placed, then balances on top a kitchen

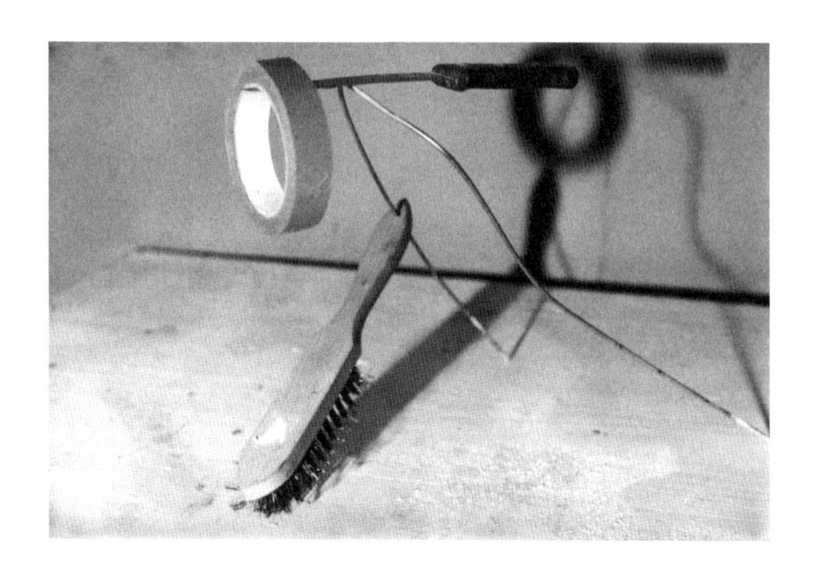

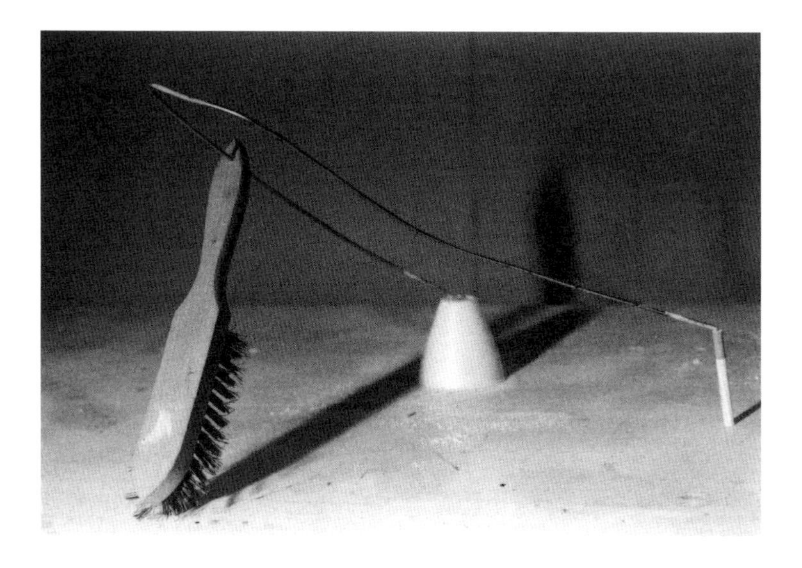

Chinese Character, photograph, 1984–86.
Taking a Break, photograph, 1984–86.
(Previously titled *Chinese Symbol* and
The Pause.)

knife counter-weighted by a roll of tape. Even the domestic arrangement of the Pear household I discussed earlier can be seen to be no more than a point along an ongoing process of metamorphosis, a development of the construction of the work *Melancholy, longing, strategy, tactics, fulfilment. A cycle.* that in turn becomes a constituent part of the yet-more-complex assembly, *The Conspiracy*. As Focillon remarked, in a manner that now seems uncannily prescient, such work 'does not occur on the spur of the moment, but results from a long series of experiments. To speak of the life of forms is inevitably to invoke the idea of succession.'[16]

If movement is implied in the teetering accumulations to be found in *Equilibres*, it is made joyously, clatteringly explicit in *The Way Things Go*. Shot over many months in an empty warehouse studio in Zürich, this 16mm film, just under 30 minutes in duration, is clearly related to the series of photographs the artists had made just previously. As the writer Patrick Frey, a long-time friend of the artists, has pointed out, the 'potential energy slumbering as latent threat in *Equilibres* has, so to speak, been expanded and translated into action in the film.'[17] David Weiss described this process of realisation similarly:

First there were the Equilibres. *We were sitting in a bar somewhere and playing around with the things on the table, and we thought to ourselves, this energy of never-ending collapse – because our construction stood for a moment and then collapsed before we built it up again – should be harnessed and channelled in a particular direction.*[18]

Many of the objects — or rather, the types of objects — featured in the film are familiar from *Equilibres*, although of course the very nature of film has allowed the artists to use movement and its effects far more extensively than was possible within the photographs in the series (such as the leaf being blown by a fan against a wire loop in *The Experiment*, or the *tsss* of gas that one suddenly becomes aware of in *The Fart*). And so, rather than trying to present a unified presence to the camera as they did in the photographs — as though standing still, holding their breath, trying not to blink — the objects are here able to follow their own inclinations (literally so in a couple of cases, when tyres and then sections of cardboard tubing roll up slopes and ladders), reacting to the situations in which they find themselves, situations that they themselves help bring about. And so the things are held in anticipation, waiting their turn, and then they go, one after the other: bags spin, tyres roll, ladders stagger, carpet rolls, chairs fall, fuses catch, fireworks blow, froth bubbles and bubbles froth. Everywhere things are transformed into actions, nouns become verbs. Things spark, things flame, things balloon, things roll; things thing, doing their thing and other things' things too.

Of course, these things are not separate, but rather connected, one leading to another, bumping, knocking, prodding, blowing, releasing. The great German engineer Franz Reuleaux, the 'father of kinematics', defined the machine in 1875 as 'a combination of resistant bodies, assembled in such a manner that, by their means and by certain determinant motions, the mechanical forces of nature are compelled to do the work.'[19] While the underlying principles might be the same, the machine we see in operation in *The Way Things Go* bears little relation to the finely crafted cast-iron and -bronze kinematic mechanisms made by Gustav Voight as working three-dimensional illustrations of Reuleaux's principles.[20] Rather, one might be reminded more readily of the contraptions of the English illustrator William Heath Robinson (1872–1944) – elaborate, often rickety contrivances powered by kettles or heated by candles, and often overseen by men in overalls, balding and bespectacled.[21]

Heath Robinson's illustrations are in one respect whimsical reactions to the rapid mechanisation of society at the turn of the twentieth century, not only in the means of production, but also in what was being produced: new consumer items such as gramophones, vacuum cleaners and cars. Standardised automated manufacturing processes had been in use since at least the sixteenth century – it was said that visiting dignitaries to Venice's *arsenale* were invited then to observe the delivery of raw materials before dining, only to see the completed, fully armed ship sail away at the end of their meal – but it was the pioneering work of Frederick Winslow Taylor (1856–1915) that has perhaps had the most profound effect on the increasing mechanisation of society, and some might argue the consolidation of a technocracy as well.[22] Combining a slide-rule and a stopwatch – often timing movements down to ten-thousandths of an hour – with guess-work and no little stubbornness, it was Taylor's

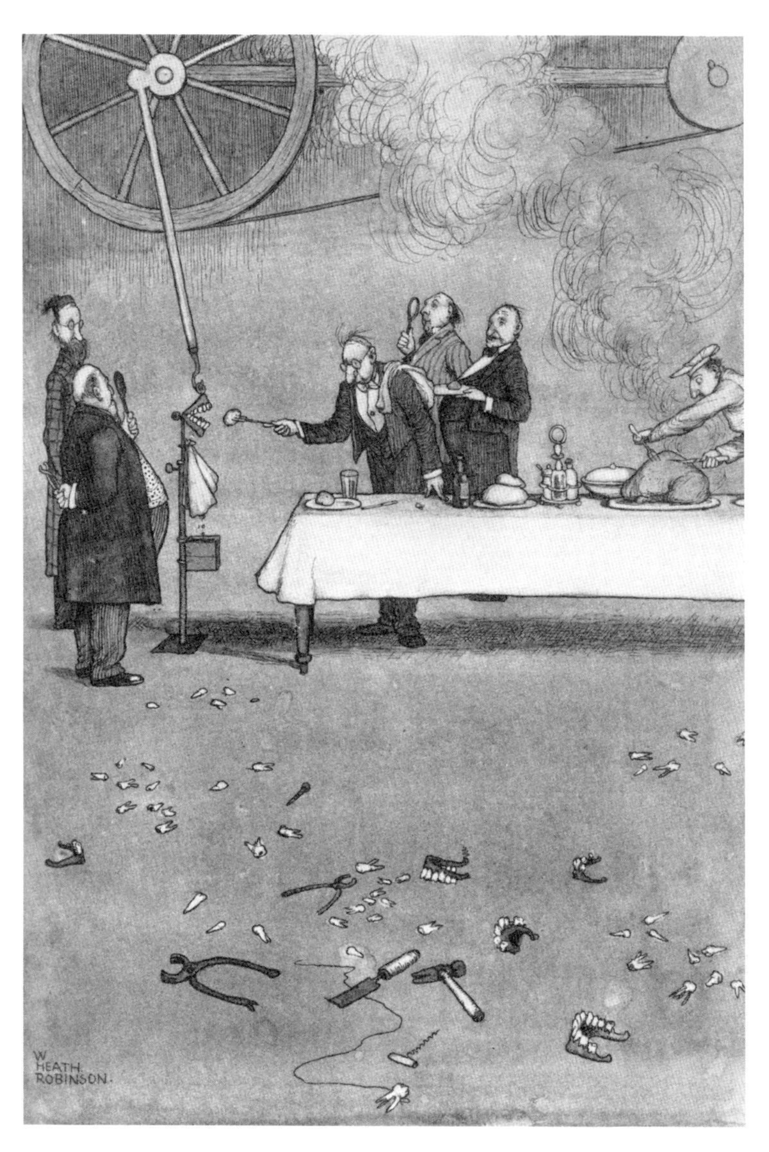

William Heath Robinson, *Testing Artificial Teeth in a Modern Tooth Works*, lithograph, from *The Sketch*, 14 March, 1909. Courtesy the estate of W.H. Robinson, © Pollinger/*The Illustrated London News* Picture Library.

firm intention to extract the maximum possible benefit from the classical economic principle of the division of labour. In 1911, some 13 years after he began developing his theories, Taylor decided to compile them into a single volume, *The Principles of Scientific Management*; within a few years, the book had been translated into Chinese, Italian, Russian, Japanese, French, German, Spanish and even that other model of universal efficiency, Esperanto. All over the world, those who ran factories (or indeed countries) read: 'In the past the man has been first. In the future the System must be first.' It is perhaps no great surprise to learn that Hitler was an admirer, as were Eichmann and Mussolini; Lenin and Stalin, too. As we can read in Yevgeny Zamyatin's great dystopian novel *We*, completed in 1921 and the model for Aldous Huxley's *Brave New World* (1932) and George Orwell's *1984* (1948):

Yes, this Taylor was, beyond a doubt, the greatest genius the ancients had. True, he had not attained the final concept of extending his method until it took in the entire life-span, every step, and both night and day — he had not been able to integrate his system from the first hour to the twenty-fourth. But just the same, how could the ancients have written whole libraries about some Kant or other, and yet barely noticed Taylor, the prophet who had been able to look ten centuries hence?[23]

It is somewhat ironic that while many factory workers were tormented by the thought of becoming merely cogs in the machine, the same was true of Taylor; a terrible insomniac, his fitful sleep was often disturbed by a recurring nightmare in which he found himself trapped within a maze of machinery — Chaplin's later nightmare of *Modern Times* (1936) had already been dreamt by the man perhaps most responsible for it.[24]

Clearly, not everyone was sympathetic to the increasingly mechanistic nature of modern life, and for every latter-day Newton coldly measuring out the Universe, there was a new-born Blake ready to reject such an orderly vision.[25] But whereas the Romantics turned their backs on the rationality of the Enlightenment and looked outward to Nature, or inward to the landscapes of the imagination, many artists of the early twentieth century responded in ways that might initially be seen as rather equivocal. (Of course some, most notably the Italian Futurists, embraced the new technologies wholeheartedly, although the mechanised slaughter of World War I changed the minds of most of those whom it did not actually kill.) In October 1912, Duchamp, Fernand Léger and Constantin Brancusi visited the Salon de la Locomotion Aérienne, and according to Léger's later account:

[Duchamp] *was walking among the motors and propellers without saying a word. Then he suddenly turned to Brancusi: 'Painting's washed up. Who'll do any better than that propeller? Tell me, can you do that?' He was very taken with these precise things.*[26]

Duchamp's supposed remark — he could not recall making it, when asked years later — has been taken as evidence of his enthusiasm for the machine aesthetic.

However, for all the devices to be found within his *oeuvre*, one cannot really consider him a committed believer, and his comment to Brancusi might be better understood as *blague*, deadpan and critical.[27] The elements within the Bachelors' domain of the *Large Glass*, while mechanical, are not machine-made — and those found in the upper section of the *Bride* are far more biomorphic — while the coffee- and chocolate-grinders to be found in his paintings, and the ready-made objects that followed them, are hardly examples of the most advanced technologies of the time. If, as the historian Linda Dalrymple Henderson has exhaustively demonstrated, Duchamp *was* interested in 'the most recent data of science' (to quote André Breton) — whether X-rays, radioactivity, the exploitation of electromagnetic waves or the more abstract explorations of non-Euclidean geometries — then it was in the manner of his favourite writers, such as Alfred Jarry and Roussel, who were similarly engaged in using such knowledge against itself in order to create a 'playful physics'.[28] The results, of course, were absurd and not without humour, even if the joke was often somewhat hidden; when Duchamp created his first 'assisted readymade' in 1913 by placing a bicycle wheel (*roue*) on a stool (*selle*), this combinatory work must surely have been an hommage to the author of *Impressions d'Afrique*.[29]

In his study of Roussel, the pioneering French psycho-analyst Pierre Janet referred on several occasions to the unusual nature of his patient's aesthetic theories: 'The work must contain nothing real, no observations of the world or the mind, nothing but completely imaginary combinations.'[30] While it is difficult to know how to conceive of such a work — neither of the world nor of the mind — especially when situated within the practice of someone renowned both for imitation and the extraordinary detail of his description, there is a sense here of *a world created anew*, and I think that this sense of a world created anew is particularly strong in Fischli and Weiss's *The Way Things Go*. Thinking back to that first screening at the ICA, just the year after it had been made, I recall thinking how timeless it seemed — or rather, that it seemed not of the time in which it was made, and in which I was watching it. Undoubtedly, part of this is due to the rather simple and everyday objects that are used throughout the film, the chairs and tables, ladders and tyres, as though taken from the illustrations in a book of children's vocabulary. But my difficulty in being able to place the film historically was due not simply to the nature of these objects, which could have come from almost any time during the twentieth century, but rather to the fact that the work seemed to be about history itself. At first a parable of the twentieth century, an age of civilisation and barbarism, the work seemed then to shift in perspective, as if seen through a '*Vertigo* effect', becoming the story of our modernity, of being modern.[31] Then with another shift, it became the story of our post-Enlightenment age; shifting yet again, it broadened toward a tale of human history; until, frighteningly, bewilderingly, this film of kettles and balloons, candles and jugs, appears to become about the whole of time. It seemed then, and seems now, to be at once pre-historic and post-apocalyptic; more than this, it seems to be both an anticipation of the birth of time and a memory of its end. But where does that place us?

When the film begins, there is nothing, only indistinct tones and forms moving across the screen; a rustling noise can be heard, although it also is indistinct. After a few seconds, the camera moves backward and the indistinct resolves itself: a black plastic bag, full though seeming to lack weight, is hanging (but from what?) and spinning. Below it, a tyre stands at the top of a slightly inclined piece of orange-coloured board, with a small strip of wood held in place by two clamps preventing it from rolling down. As the bag revolves and unwinds, it drops slightly, until eventually its base grazes the top of the tyre, catching it just enough to nudge it over the wooden strip, thereby releasing it to roll down the shallow slope and into the arrangements further on. But let us go backward for a moment, if we can, and contemplate this bag a little longer. It is an interesting shape with which to begin, I think; although obviously somewhat misshapen, with a flat-tish base and outcrops and depressions around its form, the bag does appear reasonably spherical, an effect that is further suggested by its continuous rotation, and the circle of tyre below it is perhaps a rationalisation of that which hangs above. Seeing this black, barren form spinning emptily in space like this, am I alone in thinking of it as a planet, or of something that might become one, perhaps even our own? Is this its beginning?

Perhaps it is something even more primal than the beginning of the world. In the fourth century BCE, Archytas of Tarentum wrote a treatise on place, only fragments of which now survive:

Since everything that is in motion is moved in some place, it is obvious that one has to grant priority to place, in which that which causes motion or is acted upon will be. Perhaps thus it is the first of all things, since all existing things are in place or not without place.[32]

Of course, there are many different accounts of cosmogenesis, but none of them are the simple recounting of events in time; they presuppose a form of temporality, of before and after the act of creation, but these must be considered as events that are taking place, and taking place in place. What is required is not just a place in which things can be created, but a place for creation itself; as the philosopher Edward S. Casey has remarked, 'To create "in the first place" is to create *a first place*.'[33] Rarely, if ever, is anything created *ex nihilo*, out of nothing; as Lucretius stated, *ex nihilo nihil fit*, from nothing can nothing come. Even the *Book of Genesis*, contrary to popular belief, supports such a statement:

In the beginning God created the heavens and the earth. The earth was without form and void, and darkness was upon the face of the deep; and the Spirit of God was moving over the face of the waters.
—Genesis 1: 1—2

As Casey argues, not only does 'the deep' pre-exist the act of creation, but it already possesses a face; this face is not simply amorphous either, but already has a sense of identity, 'the face of the waters', and is substantial enough to be moved over. 'In the beginning, then, was an elemental mass having sufficient density and shape to be counterposed to the movement of the spirit [...] of God.'[34] What we are considering, then, is not the nothing of an absolute void, but rather 'nothing substantial', the void as a form of chaos – that is, of an emerging order.

Is it too much to consider the artists' studio as such a void, a place that creates the place that is art? (As Focillon points out, while a work of art is situated in space, 'it will not do to say it simply exists in space: a work of art treats space according to its own needs, defines space and even creates such space as may be necessary to it.')[35] The void, place and the artists' studio are all arenas for the appearance of bodies (in Casey's phrase), and therefore also for the events that these bodies may then bring about, or are subject to subsequently. While we might therefore consider these bodies as the art objects, or the objects that make up the work of art, these bodies must be situated somewhere, in a place, and this place is called art; the studio as a void, 'a precreationist entity', is what brings this place into being.[36] As Fischli and Weiss had to find a studio especially in which to make *The Way Things Go*, one immense enough, empty enough, in which to bring it about, the sense of void, of a creative void, is particularly strong. But how might the void bring about place, and place then bring about bodies — or the studio bring about art, and then art bring about artworks? I think it is possible to get a sense of this primal act at the very beginning of the film, although it might be useful first to consider one more example given by Casey, of a Jicarilla Apache creation tale:

In the beginning nothing was here where the world now stands; there was no ground, no earth — nothing but Darkness, Water and Cyclone. There were no people living. Only the Hactcin [personifications of the powers of objects and natural forces] *existed. It was a lonely place.*[37]

In the beginning there is nothing, and then there is 'nothing but'; from the void there emerges nothing but three natural things and several distinct and identifiable forces. There is still not much — only these things — and neither are there people, but there is enough for a sense of loneliness to emerge also. Certainly this is not plenitude, but the shift from nothing at all to something is a momentous one.

As I've suggested, I think that such a shift, small but fundamental, occurs at the beginning of *The Way Things Go*. Let me recall how I described it previously: 'When the film begins, there is nothing, only indistinct tones and forms moving across the screen.' Earlier, such a description would no doubt have seemed quite unremarkable and been passed over quickly, but in light of my subsequent consideration of the void, perhaps it is now possible to become aware of the important shifts that are taking place here (indeed, of place taking *its* place)

— of there being nothing, and then nothing but 'indistinct tones and forms'. What follows afterward, as the camera pulls back to reveal the spinning bag, is a process of increasing differentiation, of separation. Almost every story of creation depends on such differentiation, of the land from the sky, of light from dark, of day from night. This is chaos in its true sense of being an opening between things — etymologically linked to *chasm* — rather than our more modern sense of a scene of disorder. Indeed, it is chaos as an emerging order, the first stage of creation, and that which makes possible the order that comes after. This is the process underway, already underway, at the beginning of this film; from an indistinct nothingness, something comes into being. It has an edge, an outline, and therefore there is also something that it is not, as well as something that it is. And then there is the tyre, its shape empty but also infinite; a shape that is reminiscent of the rotating of the more formless bag above it — suggesting the existence of other forms, as Focillon might have had it — but different from it, as though it has undergone a process of metamorphosis and become increasingly what it is, and less and less what it is not. And then, at the beginning of the world, a bin bag spins and a tyre rolls down a slope.

Is there any way in which we might know what will follow next? We are certainly familiar with basing our future predictions, our sense of what comes after, on what has come before, but in this instance there is no before; what we are considering here appears to be the very beginning of things. In his extremely influential but controversial book *L'Évolution créatrice* (1907; published in English as *Creative Evolution*, 1911), the French philosopher Henri Bergson developed a theory of philosophy in which the mechanism for evolution was provided by the *élan vital*, or 'vital impetus', further developing the importance of duration, or *durée*, in our experience of time and in the creative process. Bergson considers the creation of a portrait thus:

The painter is before his canvas, the colours are on the palette, the model is sitting – all this we see, and also we know the painter's style: do we foresee what will appear on the canvas? We possess the elements of the problem; we know in an abstract way, how it will be solved, for the portrait will surely resemble the model and surely resemble also the artist; but the concrete solution brings with it that unforeseeable nothing which is everything in a work of art. And it is this nothing that takes time.[38]

If we assume that the artist is not merely undertaking a relatively automated form of production, in which the outcome is known in advance – and so the process could not be made quicker and more 'efficient', in a Taylorist manner – then duration is an integral and irremovable element in the work's production. Even if the actual physical 'work' seems relatively slight, in this first instance, 'it is not an interval that may be lengthened or shortened without the content being altered. The duration of his [*sic*] work is part and parcel of his work. [...] The time taken up by the invention, is one with the invention itself.'[39]

This sense of duration has little in common with what Bergson dismissed as 'spatial' accounts of time, abstracted and rationalised like the most precise of Swiss clocks.[40] In contrast to such an idea of time as discrete, Bergson considered that time could only be understood – intuited – as 'lived time', as that which we experience as a succession rather than that which we hope to isolate and understand conceptually. Quite extraordinarily, Bergson illustrates this idea by describing a process to be found within *The Way Things Go* itself:

If I want to mix a glass of sugar and water, I must, willy nilly, wait until the sugar melts. This little fact is big with meaning. For here the time I have to wait is not the mathematical time, which would apply equally well to the entire history of the material world, even if that history were spread out instantaneously in space. It coincides with my own impatience, that is to say, with a certain portion of my own duration, which I cannot protract or contract as I like. It is no longer something thought, it is something lived.[41]

In *The Way Things Go*, there are a number of occasions (after the appearance of the ejaculating watering-can, for example – a phrase I never thought I'd have to write again – or of the two kettles) where a barrier of sugar acts as a dam against frothing white liquid for a time, until it becomes saturated, dissolves and then is breached, allowing the liquid to move on. When this breakthrough might occur it is difficult to say, and there is little to do to accelerate this process, even had we been able so to intervene; like Bergson, we must wait, willy-nilly, for the sugar to melt.[42] This sense of waiting is not only crucial to how we as viewers relate to this film, as I will argue, but it also contributes much of its humour.

Despite the enormous popularity of *L'Évolution créatrice* (by 1918, the original publisher had released 21 editions of the book) and its influence on many fields (not least the arts in general, and Marcel Proust in particular), there were many who criticised it, often with vehemence. One such critic, the French philosopher Gaston Bachelard, seems particularly relevant when considering *The Way Things Go*. In early works such as *L'Intuition de l'instant* (1932) and *La Dialectique de la durée* (1950), Bachelard developed a new theory of science based on epistemological obstacles and breaks.[43] Bachelard believed that these epistemological obstacles, or unconscious patterns or structures of knowledge, were widespread within the sciences, and often hindered the development of new forms of scientific knowledge by denying the possibility of conceiving of new types of questions, let alone providing new answers. As such, Bachelard's concept of duration opposed that of Bergson's continuous, ever-flowing sense of lived time; for Bachelard, duration was multiple and discontinuous, and should be considered as a series of microevents:

When we still accepted Bergson's notion of duration, we set out to study it by trying very hard to purify and consequently impoverish duration as it is given to us [...] *Yet our efforts would always encounter the same obstacle, for we never managed to overcome the lavish heterogeneity of duration*

[...] *In due course, as one might expect, we tried to find the homogenous nature of duration by confining our study to smaller and smaller fragments. Yet we were still dogged by failure ... However small the fragment, we had only to examine it microscopically to see in it a multiplicity of events.*[44]

How, then, might we consider the sense of duration within *The Way Things Go*, particularly in relation to these two quite different concepts, Bergson's organic continuity and Bachelard's fractured discontinuity? What is interesting is that despite its very obvious breaks, the film is still considered – and often loosely described – as portraying a single ongoing event, a chain reaction. As Robert Fleck described it in his essay included in *Peter Fischli/David Weiss* (2005), *The Way Things Go*:

shows a circuit of everyday objects (tyres, boards, candles) arranged in an empty warehouse so that when the first item falls over, a chain reaction amongst the rest is triggered. Here, too, the aesthetic is simple, employing no cinematic effects. The camera moves horizontally, following the action; there is no commentary, and no human intervention. *The only trick in cinematic terms is that the film is edited at several points to create an endless sequence of cause and effect.*[45]

So there are tricks, and then no tricks, but certainly no human intervention. In his own essay in the same book, Arthur C. Danto agrees, stating that 'As artists, they are outside the system they have contrived. Or that is the impression they have sought to achieve'[46]

The qualification is important. The interventions, actually, are numerous, and usually quite obvious. Most of these are simple edits in the film — I counted at least 26, and perhaps 27, cuts in the film. Many of these are obvious, such as the dissolves on the bubbling froth that appears as a refrain throughout the film, while others are rather more hidden, clean cuts made while a piece of magnesium flares, or against a black background or a spinning black bag, that can usually only be spotted in the shift of a camera angle or a change of background. Furthermore, there are a number of more direct interventions in the process itself, incidents of *deus ex machina*, such as when a fuse is lit off-screen just after the Catherine-wheel vehicle falls bubbling and churning into a bucket of liquid, or the kettle is heated by a gas burner separate from the fire surrounding it. (I also have my suspicions about a firework lit on the far side of a tyre.) I want to emphasise, however, that these observations are in no way meant to lessen the value of this work, to explain how the trick's done; on the contrary, as I want to argue, the importance and wonder of this work lies in the fact that knowing of these acts seems to increase the work's power to fascinate and involve the viewer, rather than decrease it.[47] Nevertheless, it is important to note these artistic interventions — either within the working of the process or in its subsequent representation — when certain philosophic or theological points are made based on observations of the film, and particularly when the observations are, at best, somewhat contradictory and difficult to reconcile (much like the work they seem to describe).

Given the epochal sweep that might be claimed for this film, could we consider it to be 'epic'? Danto certainly considered it to be 'an epic of some kind', although we are left to wonder precisely which kind.[48] In his essay 'Epic and Novel', the Russian critic Mikhail Bakhtin suggests that the epic has these characteristics:

The world of the epic is the national heroic past: it is a world of 'beginnings' and 'peak times' in the national history, a world of fathers and founders of families, a world of 'firsts' and 'bests'. The important point here is not that the past constitutes the content of the epic. The formally constitutive feature of the epic as a genre is rather the transferral of a represented world into the past, and the degree to which this world participates in the past. The epic was never a poem about the present, about its own time (one that became a poem about the past only for those that came later). The epic, as the specific genre known to us today, has been from the beginning a poem about the past, and the authorial position immanent in the epic and constitutive for it (that is, the position of the one who utters the epic word) is the environment of a man speaking about a past that is to him inaccessible, the reverent point of view of a descendent.[49]

It is not simply that the events within an epic take place in the distant past, as this would then allow any suitably aged narrative to be characterised as such, even if it were set in a period contemporaneous with its production. Rather, the age of the epic must be completely discontinuous with our own; we cannot hope to walk back along history's path and find it there awaiting us. It is a time already finished, perhaps always already finished; it is complete, and in not needing anything to be added, it remains inaccessible for all those who come after. Indeed, for the epic there is no after, no sense of another time at all, for it is the 'absolute past' and remains absolutely closed. Even as we hope to take from it — wisdom, understanding, perhaps even a sense of identity — it remains the same, complete and indifferent.

As the title of Bakhtin's essay suggests, for him it is the novel that might be considered to be the antithesis of the epic, and while I would hesitate to characterise *The Ways Things Go* in this way, like many other works in Fischli and Weiss's practice (*Suddenly This Overview* and the 1995 Venice videos not least among them), it certainly shares much with the 'anti-epic'. It is perhaps its sense of time — a time that is ongoing and incomplete — that most obviously distinguishes Fischli and Weiss's film from the epic as it is here defined. As Bakhtin describes it, the epic is 'as closed as a circle; inside it everything is finished, already over. There is no place in the epic world for any open-endedness, indecision, indeterminacy. There are no loopholes through which we glimpse the future; it suffices unto itself, neither supposing any continuation nor requiring it.'[50] Clearly, one could not say this of *The Way Things Go*, a work whose every moment presupposes subsequent moments, whose every act brings about further acts, as if the marble sphere of the epic, perfect and impenetrable, has been picked up and rolled along the debris-strewn floor of history. Thereby the epic — if not necessarily breached, or denied its formal

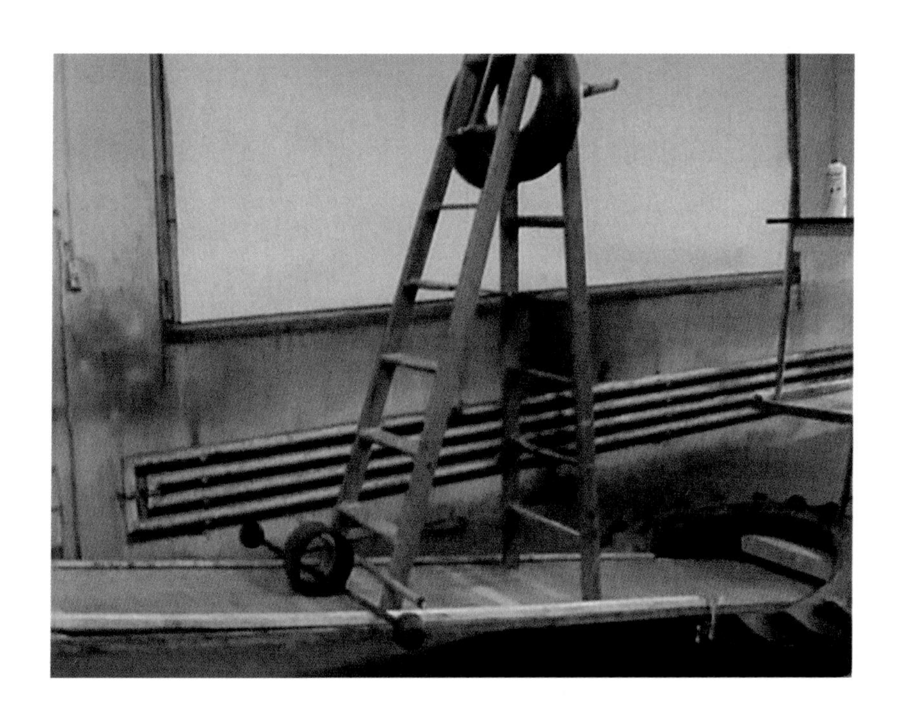

1.—19. Stills from *The Way Things Go*, 16mm colour film, 30mins, 1987.

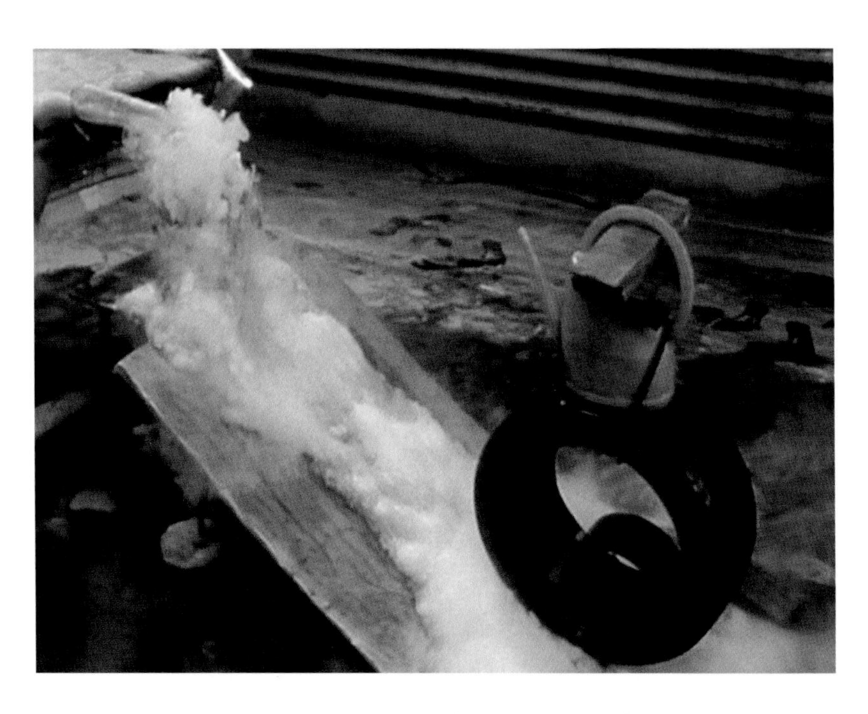

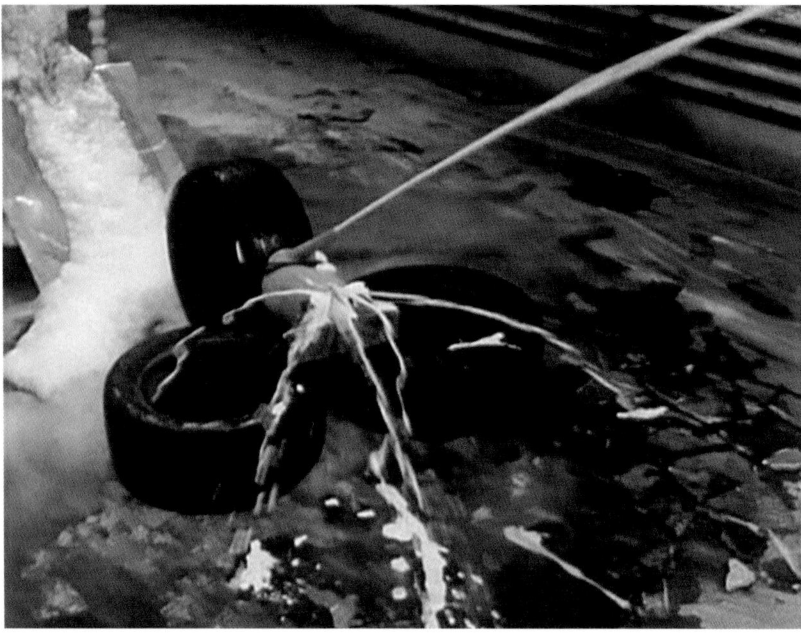

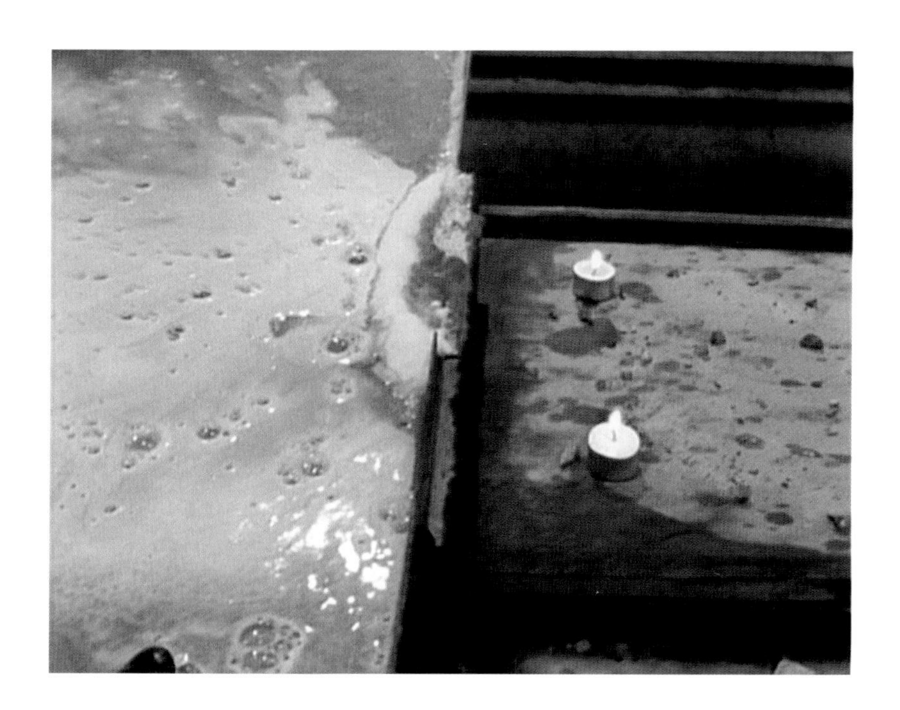

2.—4.

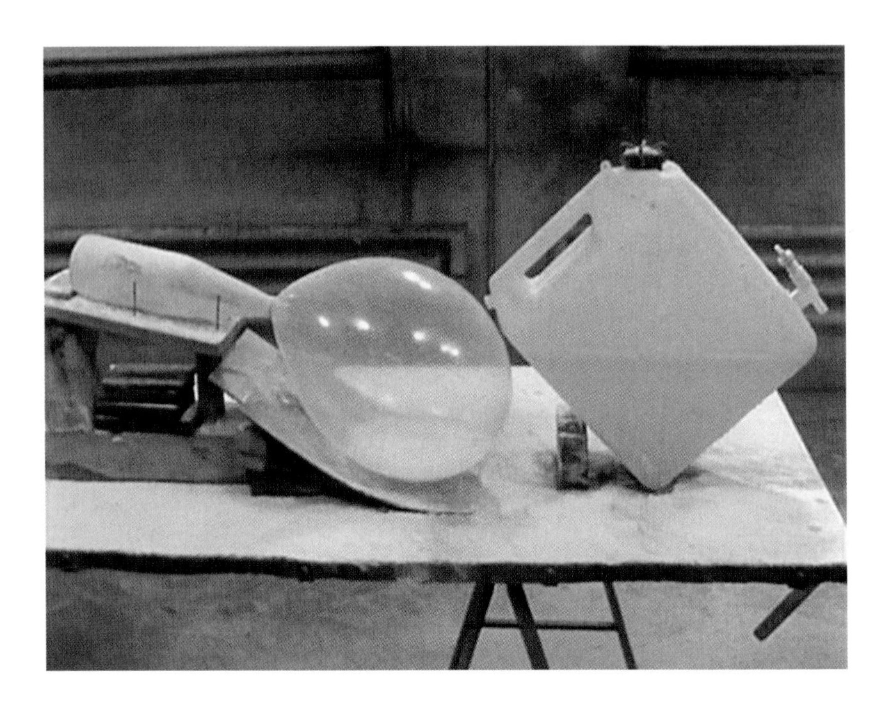

5.

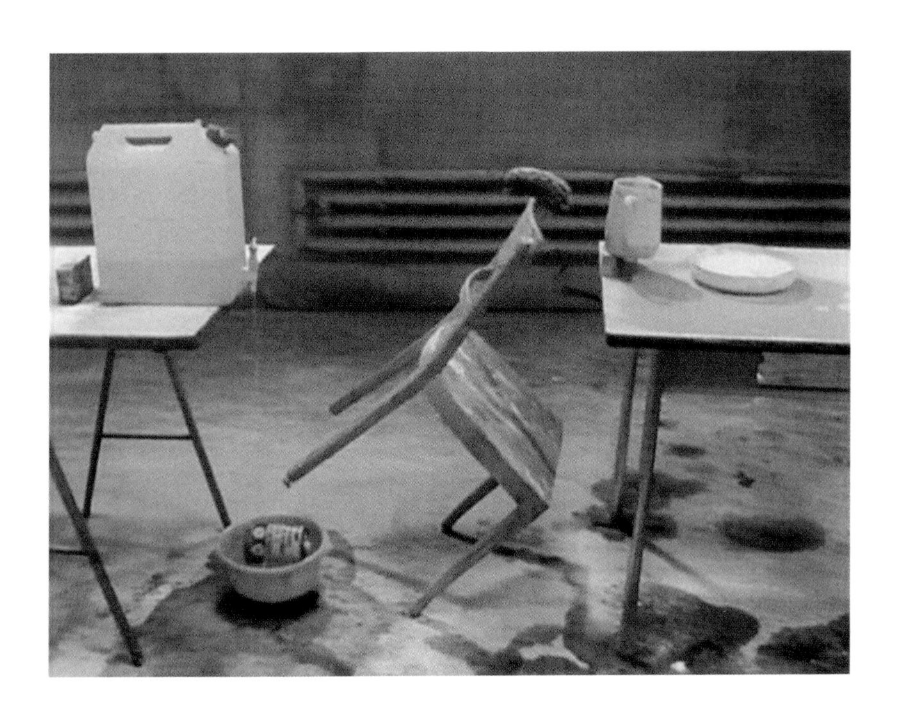

6.

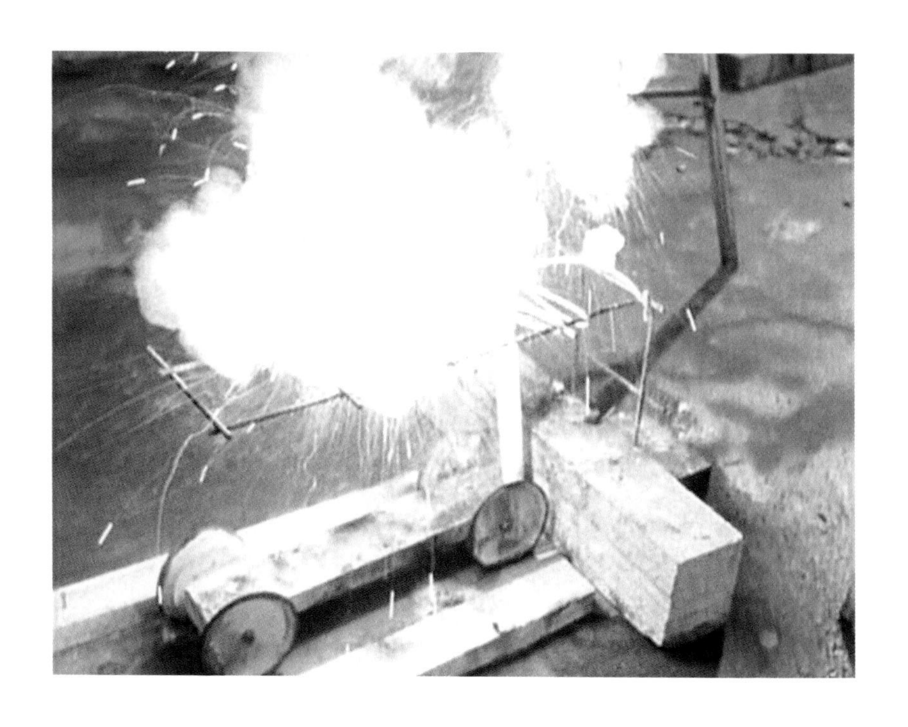

7.

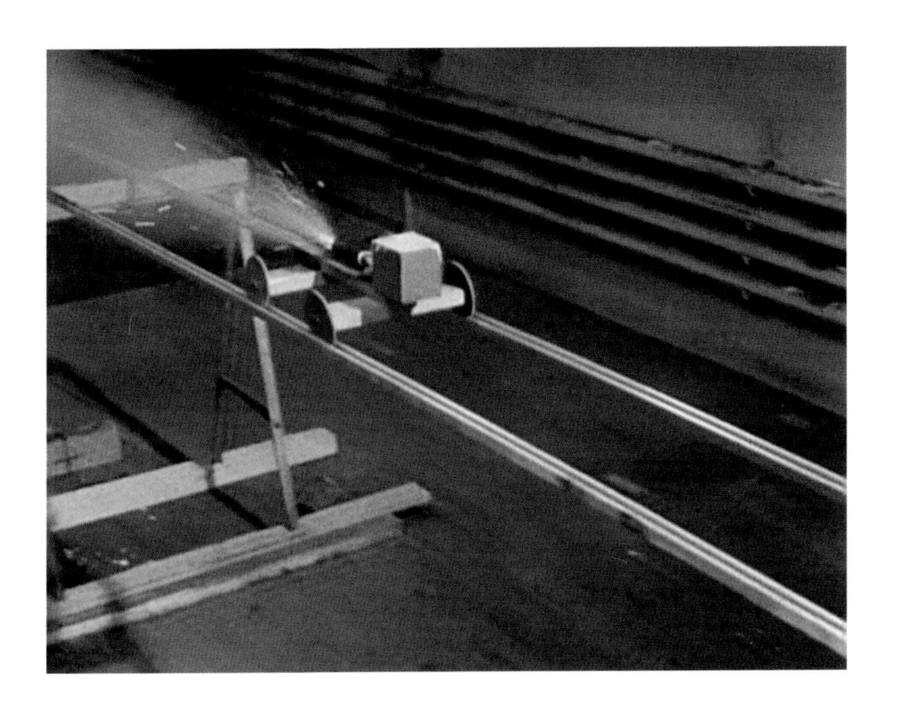

8.

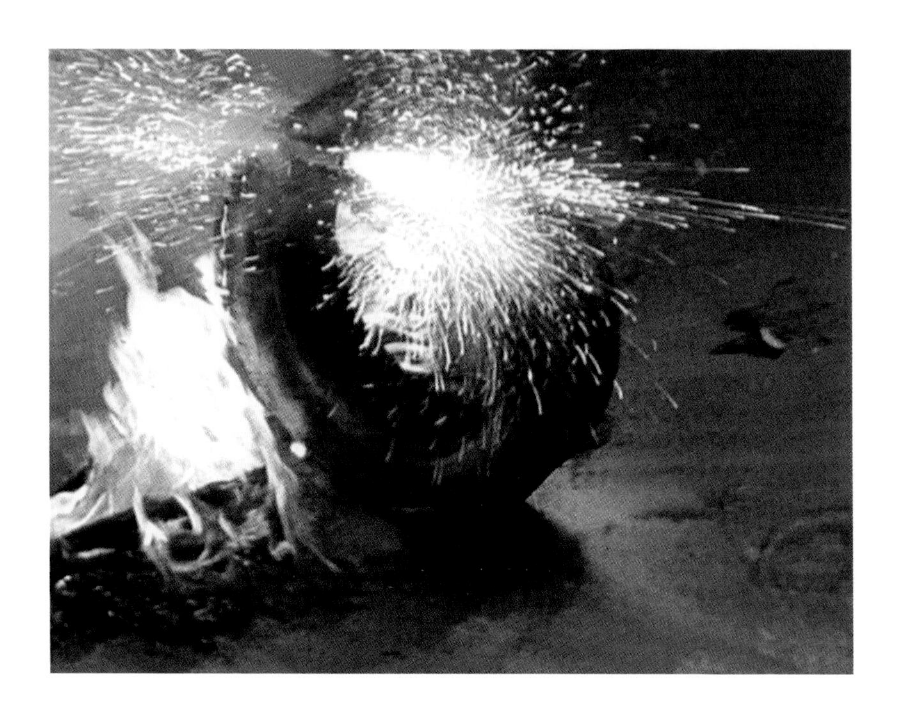

9.

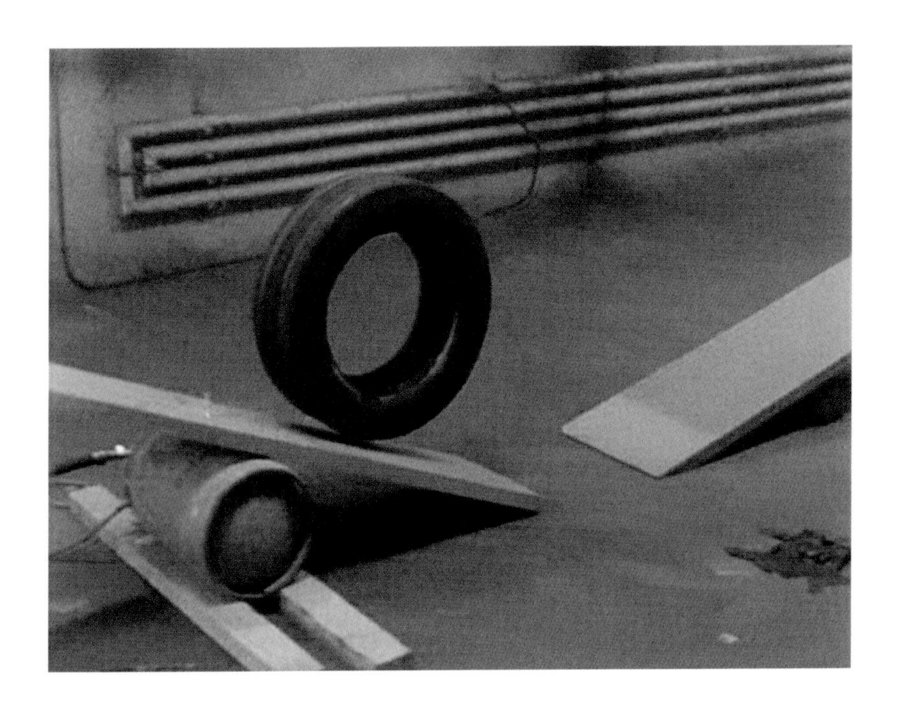

10.

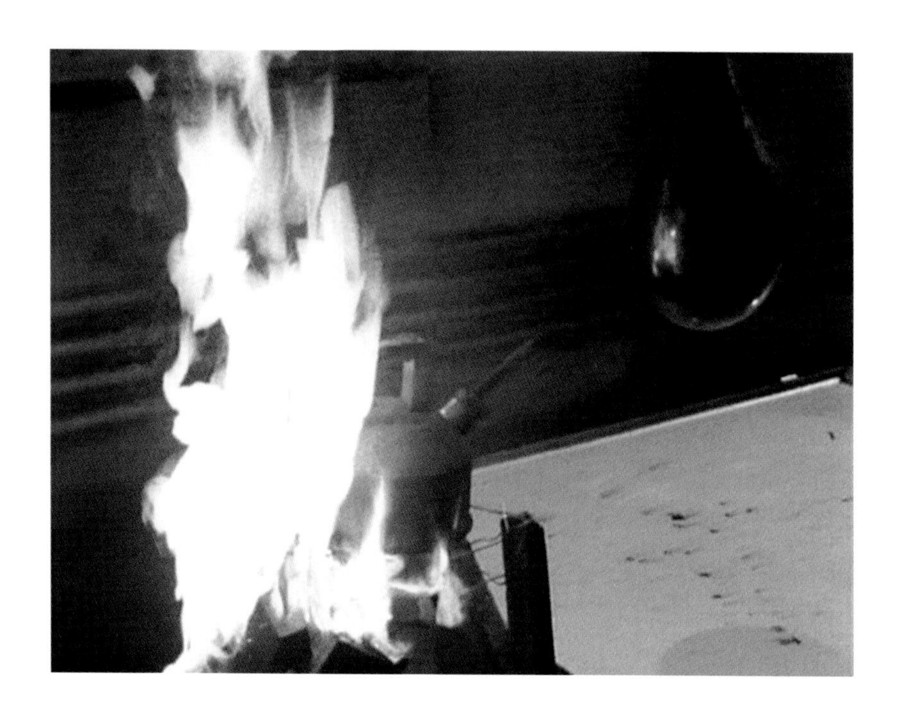

11.

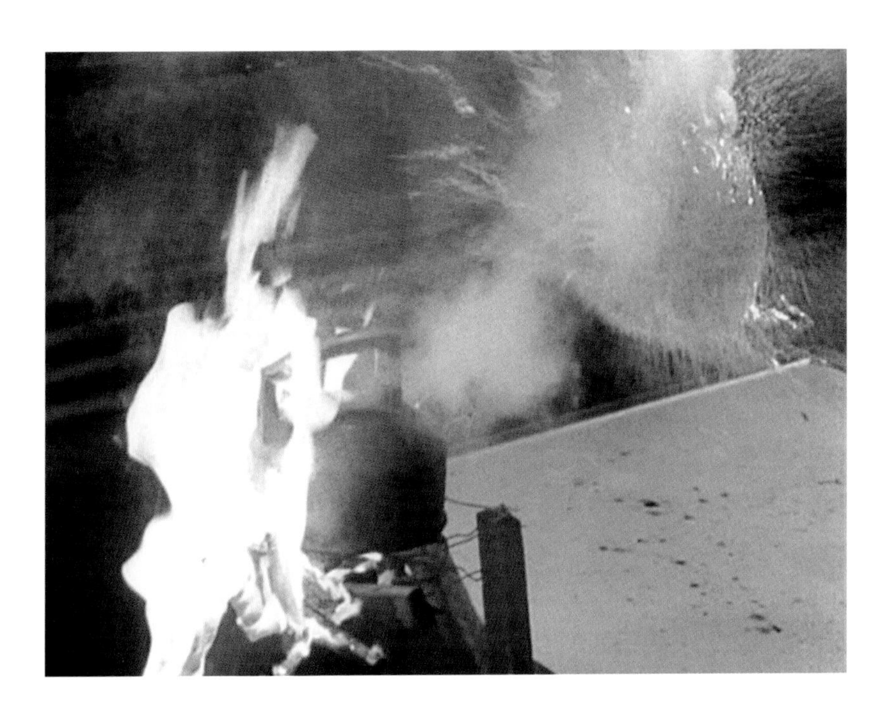

12.

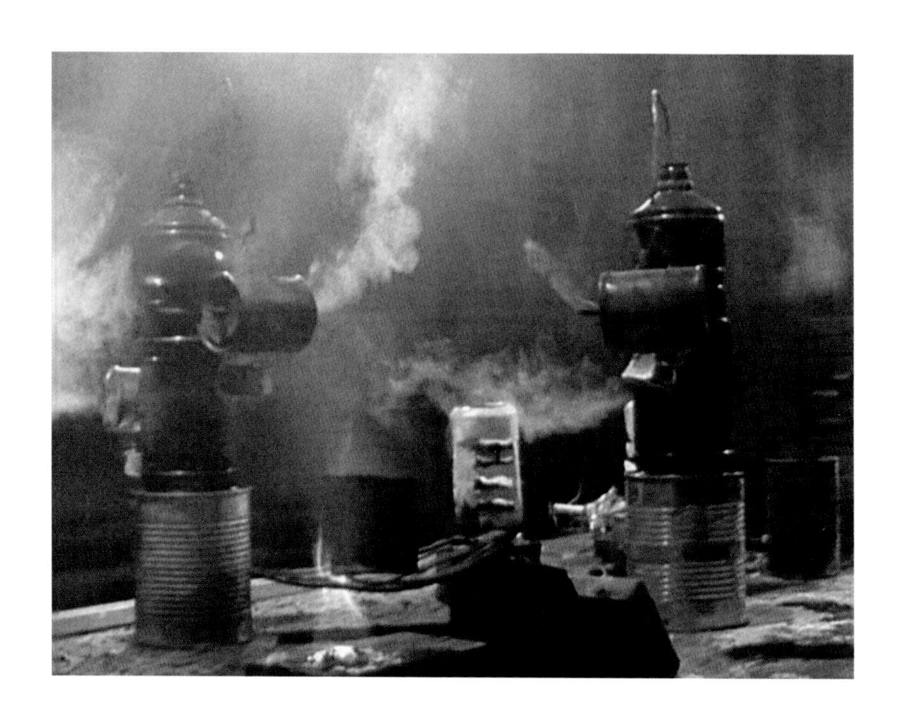

13.—15.

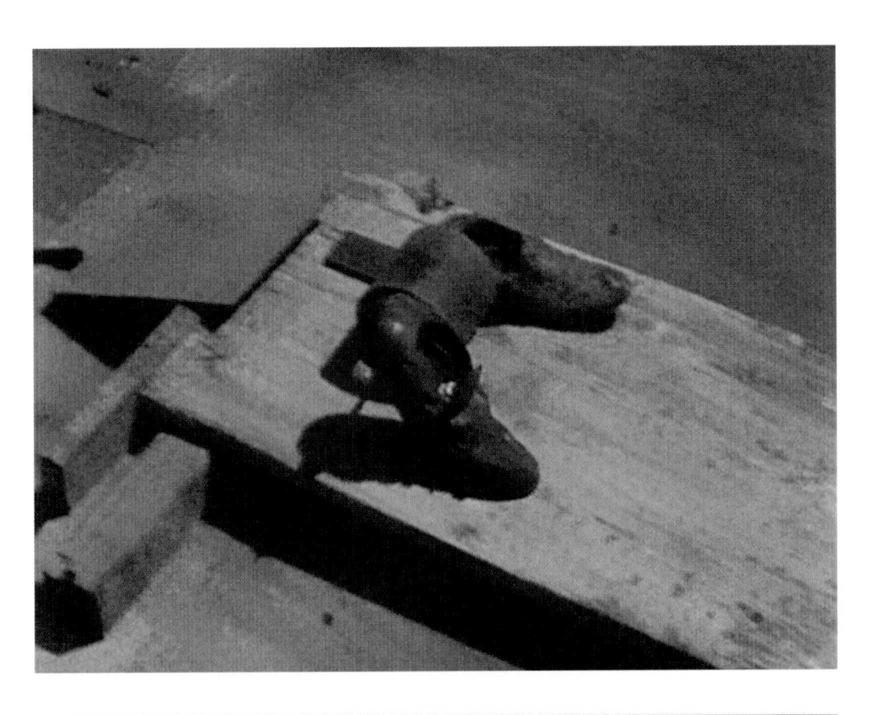

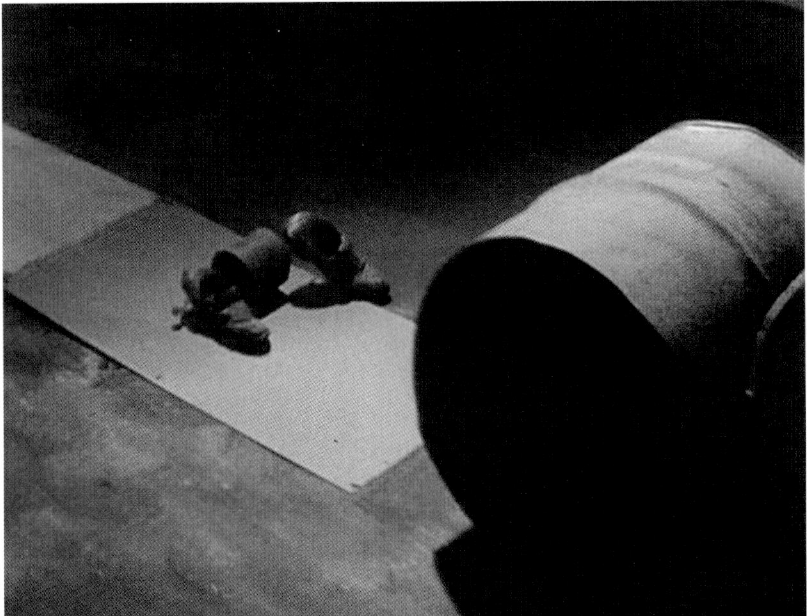

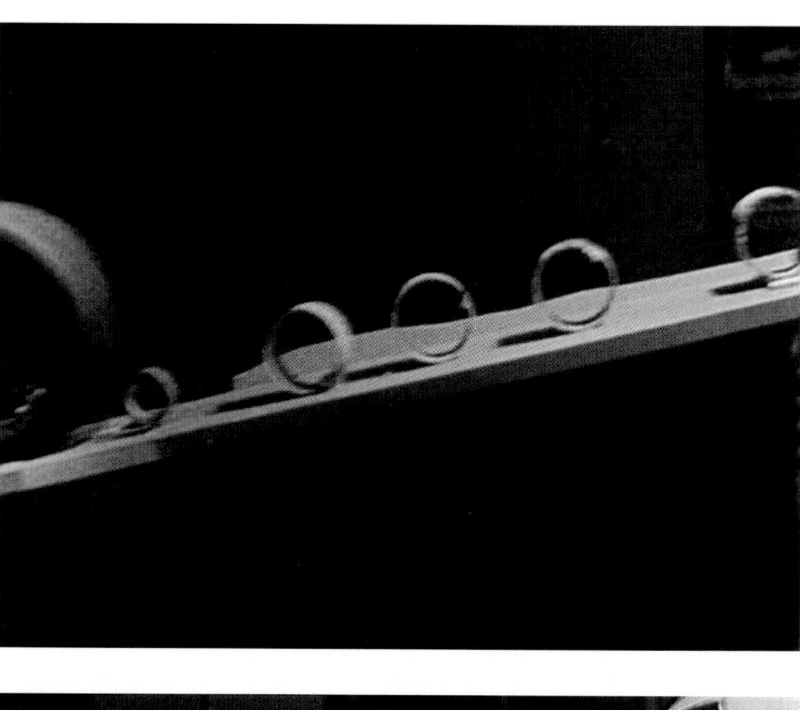

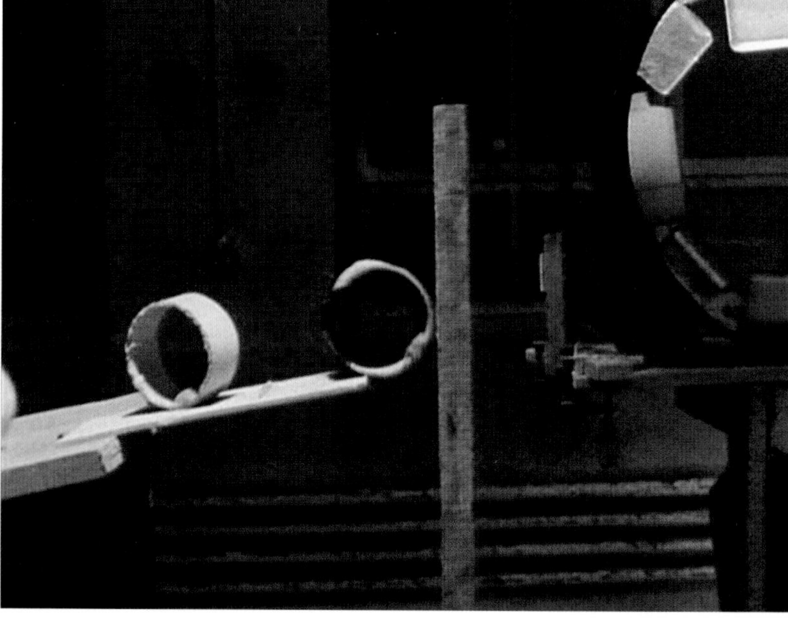

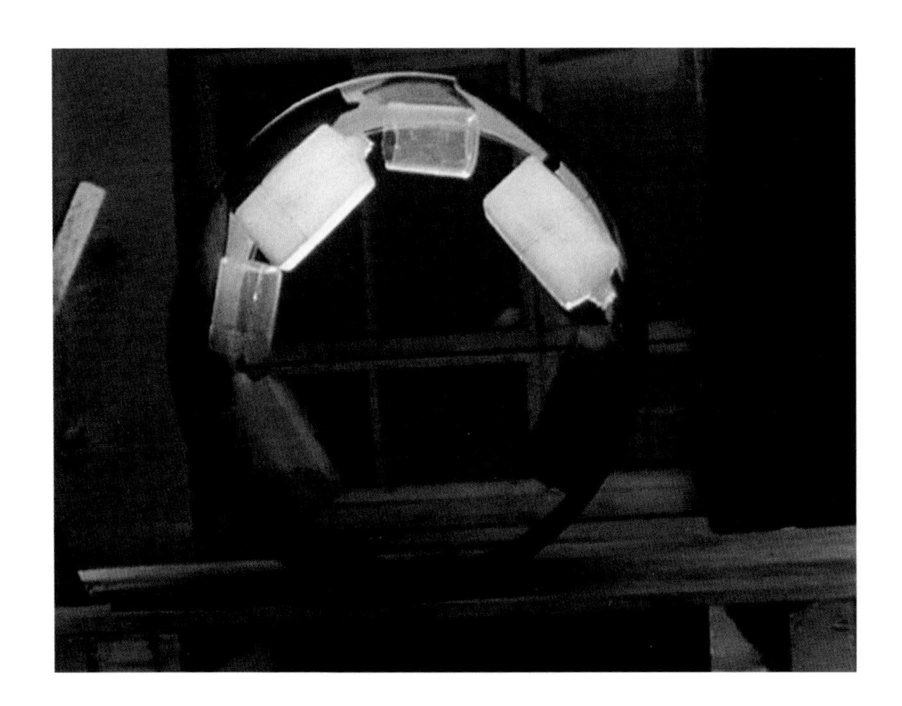

16.–18.

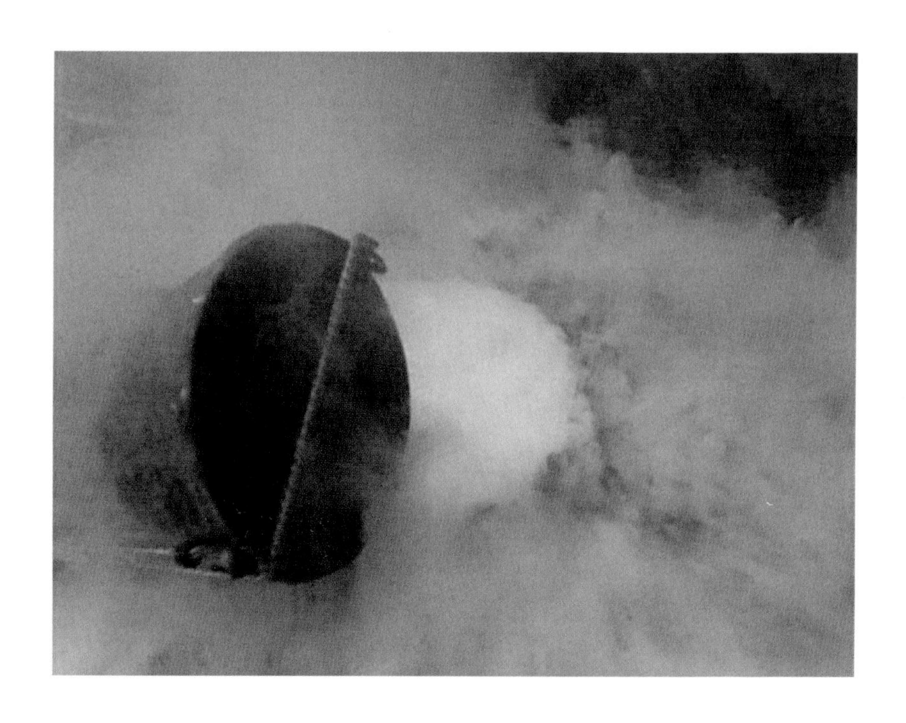

19.

integrity — is transformed into an historical agent, into which things can collide, and by which things can be collided against. It becomes a part of time, not apart from it.

Perhaps we might think of the epic within *The Way Things Go* as somewhat parodic, then, 'brought low, represented on a plane equal with contemporary life, in an everyday environment, in the low language of contemporaneity'.[51] The beginning (of what? Of the film, certainly, but of everything?) as a spinning dustbin bag; a vision of a hellish place made of empty cans and bottles, spluttering and steaming. Like the remarkable carved and painted polyurethane replicants of everyday items found in works such as *Table* (1992—93) or *Room Under the Stairs* (1993), the film might be considered an *image* of that which it appears to be, rather than the thing itself. Such a work does not require a hero who is uncorrupted and unchanging for, as Bakhtin says of the parodic 'sonnets' that open *Don Quixote* (1605), it is itself '*the hero of the parody*', and can as a consequence draw on figures who are scuffed and stumbling, broken, baffled and beaten. Such a situation was described with typical beauty by Bruno Schulz:

We are not concerned with long-winded creations, with long-term beings. Our creatures will not be heroes of romances in many volumes. Their roles will be short, concise; their characters — without a background. Sometimes, for one gesture, for one word alone, we shall make the effort to bring them to life. We openly admit: we shall not insist either on durability or solidity of workmanship; our creations will be temporary, to serve for a single occasion. If they be human beings, we shall give them, for example, only one profile, one hand, one leg, the one limb needed for their role. It would be pedantic to bother with the other, unnecessary, leg. Their backs can be made of canvas or simply white-washed. We shall have this proud slogan as our aim: a different actor for every gesture. For each action, each word, we shall call to life a different human being. Such is our whim, and the world will be run according to our pleasure. The Demiurge was in love with consummate, superb, and complicated materials; we shall give priority to trash. We are simply entranced and enchanted by the cheapness, shabbiness and inferiority of material.[52]

And so the objects within *The Way Things Go* — the actors, or those that act — are no more than they need to be; if they are required to roll down a slope, then that is what they shall do, and no more. A chair tips up because it has been knocked off balance; a candle lights a fuse because it has been rolled underneath it; a pair of shoes waddle down a slope. Here there is no need for athletic bodies, for heads raised, arms outstretched, legs readied, steadied; Hermes's winged sandals are superfluous when all that is required is that a pair of trundling loafers clatter into an oil drum.

Of course, we laugh; such is the most immediate response when lofty significance stumbles and is brought low, as the reader will no doubt have discovered already. In entering the turbulent flow of time, stiff-limbed classicism loses its grace and becomes awkward and clumsy — and thereby vulnerable, as Bakhtin makes clear:

It is precisely laughter that destroys the epic, and in general destroys any hierarchical (distancing and valorised) distance. As a distanced image a subject cannot be comical; to be made comical it must be brought close. Everything that makes us laugh is close at hand, all comical creativity works in a zone of maximal proximity. Laughter has the remarkable power of making an object come up close, of drawing it into a zone of crude contact where one can finger it familiarly on all sides, turn it upside down, inside out, peer at it from above and below; break open its external shell, look into its centre, doubt it, take it apart, dismember it, lay it bare and expose it, examine it freely and experiment with it. Laughter demolishes fear and piety before an object, before a world, making of it an object of familiar contact and thus clearing the ground for an absolutely free investigation of it. Laughter is a vital factor in laying down that prerequisite for fearlessness without which it would be impossible to approach the world realistically. As it draws an object to itself and makes it familiar, laughter delivers the object into the fearless hands of investigative experiment — both scientific and artistic — and into the hands of free experimental fantasy.[53]

And so we are able to discern two distinct, albeit complementary, actions: the destruction of the elevated through laughter, and the production of laughter through the destruction of the elevated. Although both actions seem to move in contrary directions — laughter the cause in one and the effect in the other — they are related; in both cases, that which was considered in some sense superior is laid low, and brought into the realm with which we are familiar. Sometimes one cannot suppress the satisfied grin of *schadenfreude*, especially when someone more used to pronouncing on the immorality of others is found in embarrassing circumstances – the upright, uptight politician being caught playing infantilising sex games, or the priest indulging in wine that is not communal or a spirit that is not Holy – and the sense of ridicule overcomes any moral indignation.[54] Even if we find such a person reduced to our level, our mocking allows us a feeling of superiority, the feeling which, in *Leviathan* (1651), Thomas Hobbes proposed lay at the heart of all laughter: 'Sudden glory is the passion which makes all those grimaces called laughter; and it is caused either by some sudden act of their own, that pleases them; or by the apprehension of some deformed thing in another by comparison whereof they applaud themselves.'[55] Such a view is hardly surprising from someone who held that life was 'solitary, poor, nasty, brutish and short', but opposing views were developed in time. Whereas for Hobbes, society was, for the most part, a state of *bellum omnium contra omnes*, or 'the war of all against all', and our actions, however seemingly well-intentioned, were motivated by self-interest, for the philosopher Francis Hutcheson (1694–1746), one of the founders of the Scottish Enlightenment, benevolence was of equal necessity, and furthermore was a stimulus of which we could approve. In addition, he proposed a *sensus communis*, or public sense, which he considered a determination to be pleased with the happiness of others and to be uneasy at their misery.

Of course, such a strong moral sense could not countenance Hobbes's cruel mockery, and in his *Thoughts on Laughter* (first published in 1725), Hutcheson dismissed the need for us to feel superior in order to feel amusement; as he pointed out, we rarely laugh at oysters. Instead, Hutcheson suggested that:

Generally the cause of laughter is the bringing together of images which have contrary additional ideas, as well as some resemblance in the principal idea; this contrast between ideas of grandeur, dignity, sanctity, perfection, and ideas of meanness, baseness, profanity, seems to be the very spirit of the burlesque; and the greatest part of our raillery and jest is founded upon it.

We also find ourselves moved to laughter by an overstraining of wit, by bringing resemblances from subjects of quite different kind from the subject to which they are compared.[56]

Although such a basis would account for the delighted amusement we might find in the perverted moralist or the drunken priest, *viz.* the 'contrast between ideas of [...] dignity [...] and ideas of [...] baseness', the incongruity theory — or the Incongruity Tradition, as it has now become known — seems far easier to relate to that which we find humorous, especially with regard to our increasing delight in the absurd. The surprising or illogical juxtaposition of elements, or the placing of an object or person in an unexpected situation, creates an uncertainty that it appears only humour can resolve. One might think of Rat and Bear's irritable argument at the beginning of Fischli and Weiss's 1981 film

Der Geringste Widerstand (*The Least Resistance*), of Rat elaborating his aesthetic theories or Bear his existential despair; or indeed, even more simply, of the artists themselves dressing up in such cheap animal costumes and parading around Los Angeles. Of course, the contrary may occur and reality might beat us to it, producing a situation so unlikely, so unexpected, that it effectively neutralises humour; one need only recall Tom Lehrer's reported remark that satire died the day Henry Kissinger was awarded the Nobel Peace Prize.

In attempting to summarise the conservative worldview of comic books (such as *Gem* and *Magnet*) in his essay 'Boys' Weeklies', George Orwell famously suggested that 'their basic political assumptions are two: nothing ever changes, and foreigners are funny'.[57] For this Briton looking now at the work of Fischli and Weiss, and at *The Way Things Go* in particular, such assumptions could be seen to be at best only half right; actually, things do change, but these foreigners, at least, are good for a laugh. (Of course, the foreigners in the comics were to be laughed at rather than with – the excitable Frenchman or Italian, the kind-hearted but stupid Swede or Dane. Perhaps it is fortunate that the Swiss escaped such categorisation.) Humour has been a crucial, inescapable element within the artists' practice since their first collaborative work, the *Wurstserie* (*Sausage Series*) from 1979, and the sense of incongruity is obvious from the very beginning. In the ten photographs of this series, the artists seem to have wilfully ignored the exhortation made by every irritated parent to their children: *please* do not play with your food.

Actually, despite the title of the series, not all of the photographs within it contain sausages, or even food. In one such work, *Titanic*, the white plastic bottle of a liner sinks beneath the surface of the dark bathwater after seemingly colliding with the broken polystyrene-bergs that float sharp and pretend-scary on it, while in *Cavemen* a match-stick fire burns high and bright in the dulled blackness of a domestic oven, crude forms — the first art? — scratched hesitantly on the walls. But of course the sausages do appear, already funny in themselves, and now made funnier by their cooptation into scenes both tragic and trivial. In *The Accident*, a crowd of cigarette butts gathers round two sausage cars that have collided at the junction between cardboard-box buildings, while in *Fashion Show* five sausage stumps, with the smoked skins of a St. Tropez tan, parade on the pink-painted shelf beneath what seems to be a bathroom mirror, draped in cold-cuts or a twist of toilet paper. In perhaps the most wonderful work from the series, *At the Carpet Shop* — a work that never fails to raise a smile each time I look at it — a family of gherkins inspects piles of cooked-meat carpets and rugs, helped, one hopes, by the tip of white radish that can only be the sales assistant. One of the gherkins seems to be bending over to inspect the quality of one particular slice of processed meat; a smaller gherkin, presumably the child, stands a little further behind, and is, one can only assume, already a little bored. A single round slice of mortadella, broad and flecked with fat, sits richly in the centre of the shop; dog-biscuit cushions are scattered throughout.

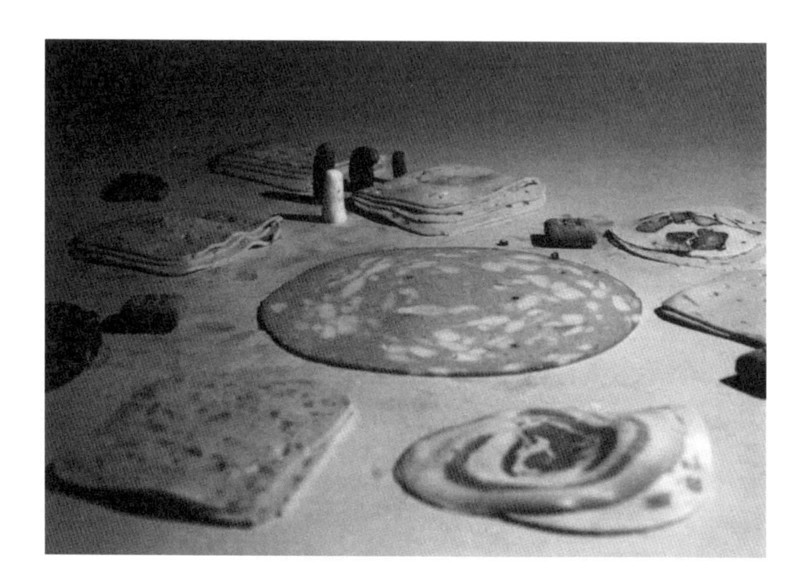

At the Carpet Shop, photograph, 1979.

Although the absurdity produced by bringing together incongruous elements has been explored by numerous thinkers since Hutcheson – Kierkegaard and Arthur Schopenhauer among them – perhaps it is the writing of Arthur Koestler that might prove most relevant here, not least because it explores the creativity of the jester, the sage and the artist, roles that I would suggest are not unfamiliar to Fischli and Weiss themselves. In *The Act of Creation* (1964), Koestler proposes that all forms of creativity, whether comic inspiration, philosophical insight or artistic originality, share a basic pattern, which he attempts to illustrate in a table reproduced on the book's frontispiece. The table consists of three untitled columns that we soon learn refer to three domains of creativity: humour, discovery and art. Each column consists of a number of words or phrases, while the words across each row are joined by two-headed arrows, so that the word in the central column, that of the 'sage', relates to both the word to its left (in the column for the 'jester'), and to the right (for the 'artist'), while these words refer back to that found in the middle. As Koestler attempts to explain it:

Each horizontal line across the triptych stands for a pattern of creative activity which is represented on all three panels; for instance: comic comparison – objective analogy – poetic image. The first is intended to make us laugh; the second to make us understand; the third to make us marvel. The logical pattern of the creative process is the same in all three cases; it consists in the discovery of hidden similarities.[58]

Although Koestler explores the pattern across different forms of creativity with typical thoroughness over nearly 500 closely typed pages, he defines it quite clearly as the 'perceiving of a situation or idea [...] in two self-consistent but habitually incompatible frames of reference', which seems to coincide quite remarkably with the incongruity theory of humour discussed earlier.[59] Koestler quotes the following joke (told to him by another Hungarian Jew, his friend the mathematician and polymath John von Neumann) by way of illustration:

Two women meet while shopping at the supermarket in the Bronx. One looks cheerful, the other depressed. The cheerful one inquires:

'What's eating you?'

'Nothing's eating me.'

'Death in the family?'

'No, God forbid!'

'Worried about money?'

'No... nothing like that.'

'Trouble with the kids?'

'Well, if you must know, it's my little Jimmy.'

'What's wrong with him then?'

'Nothing is wrong. His teacher said he must see a psychiatrist.'

Pause. 'Well, well, what's wrong with seeing a psychiatrist?'

'Nothing is wrong. The psychiatrist said he's got an Oedipus complex.'

Pause. 'Well, well, Oedipus or Shmoedipus, I wouldn't worry so long as he's a good boy and loves his mamma.'[60]

As Koestler remarks, the cheerful woman's closing statement is ruled by the logic of common sense: 'if Jimmy is a good boy and loves his mamma there can't be much wrong. But in the context of Freudian psychiatry, the relationship to the mother carries entirely different associations.'[61] An old joke, and one hardly enhanced by explanation, but for Koestler, it clearly illustrates the clash of two mutually incompatible codes or frames of reference, and the humour — such as it is — that results when what it means to love your mamma 'is made to vibrate simultaneously on two different wavelengths, as it were'. While this situation persists, and the vibrations continue, the idea 'is not merely linked to one associative context, but *bisociated* into two'.[62] For Koestler, the idea of 'bisociation' makes a clear distinction between a routine thought, taking place on a single 'plane' or associative context, and the creative act, which he suggests always operates on more than one plane. 'The former may be called single-minded, the latter a double-minded, transitory state of unstable equilibrium where the balance of both emotion and thought is disturbed.'[63] As Peter Fischli stated in a recent interview, 'Operating on two planes at once is part of our practice.'[64]

It need hardly be pointed out that one can find examples of bisociation throughout Fischli and Weiss's practice. It is apparent in their earliest collaborative work, the recently described *Sausage Series*, wherein the relative senses of tragedy or triviality – of the car crash as opposed to the fashion show, the sinking Titanic as opposed to the carpet shop – is immaterial in comparison to the fact that all of these scenarios have been staged using bits of food and household goods. Similarly, the misadventures of Rat and Bear in the two artists' films *Der Geringste Widerstand* (*The Least Resistance*, 1981) and *Der Rechte Weg* (*The Right Way*, 1983) offer numerous bisociative examples – the art-world intrigues, the murder mystery, the existential anxieties, the moral dilemmas – even if we disregard the most obvious aspects: that Rat and Bear act like people, in all their foul-mouthed irritability, regardless of their supposed animal identities. With that said, these identities are hardly meant to convince visually either, with the cheap, ill-fitting suits rendering both 'animals' the same size. Indeed, it is the poverty of the impersonation that emphasises the bisociation at work, for as Koestler remarks:

the impersonator is perceived as himself and somebody else at the same time. While this situation lasts, the two matrices [the impersonator and that which is being impersonated] *are bisociated in the spectator's mind; and while his intellect is capable of swiftly oscillating from one matrix to the other and back his emotions are incapable of following these acrobatic turns; they are spilled in the gutters of laughter as soup is spilled on a rocking ship.*[65]

The same might be said of the assemblages found in *Equilibres*, wherein the rolls of tape, washing-up bowl, and aerosol really *do* seem to become Ben Hur, or the graters, twine, bottle and other objects really do become roped mountaineers, while at the same time they are in no way transformed, remaining exactly what they are.

I think that such a process can be seen to occur quite clearly throughout *The Way Things Go*, with everyday objects removed from the everyday and performing tasks that are both the same as those they are used to – filling, falling, emptying, rolling – and different, tasks that they would and would not ordinarily do. And so, while there is usually little of interest in watching a kettle boil, here we do just that, and for some time it seems, before it screams along a rail and crashes flaming into a nearby table, or fires a point into a balloon hanging just overhead.[66] Car tyres roll, as untold millions do each day, but here they roll along horizontal ladders, or are driven by the weight of water or the eventual *pfffsssszzz* of a firework. In acting in a bisociative manner like this, on two different planes, the objects seem to enact what Jean Baudrillard, in *The System of Objects* (1968), referred to as '"functional"

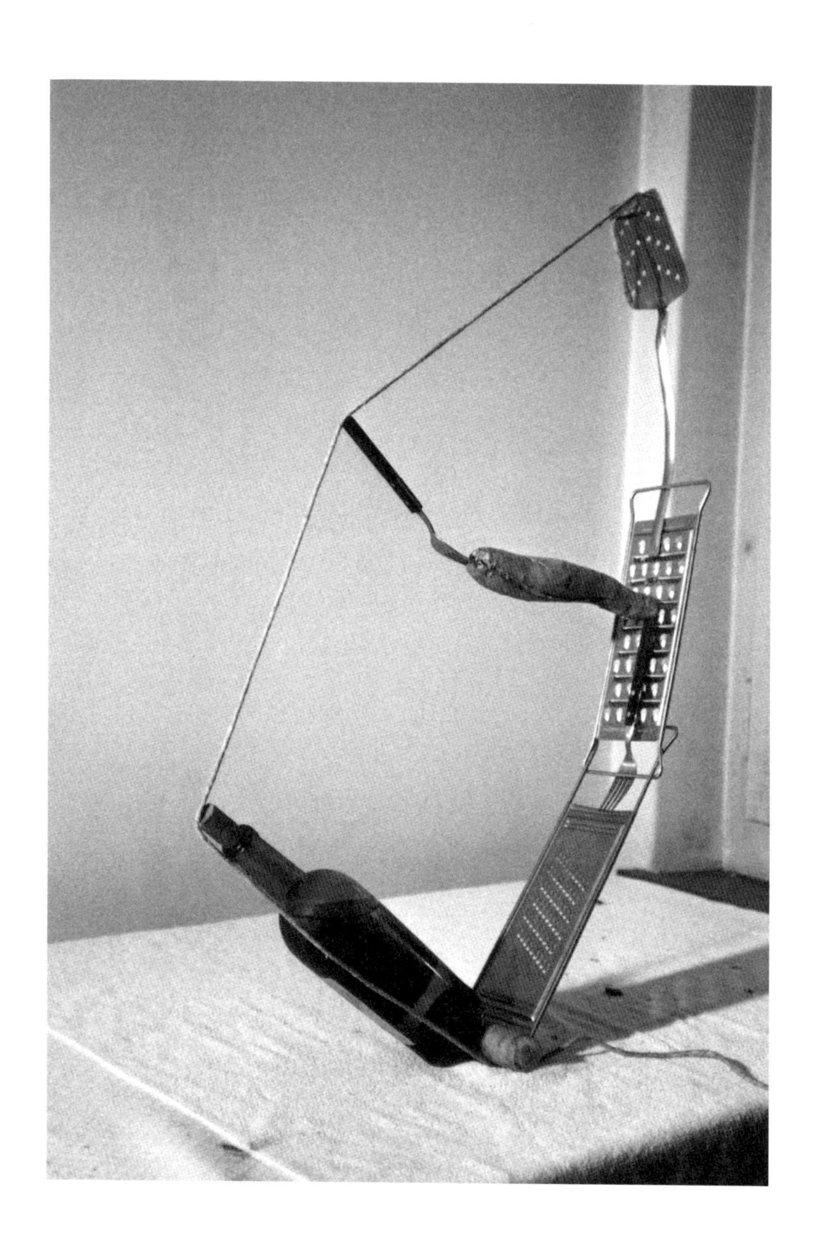

Roped Mountaineers, photograph,
1984–86.

transcendence', a process of transformation that may be threatened by an increased desire for automation and technical specialisation:

The degree to which a machine approaches perfection is thus everywhere presented as proportional to its degree of automatism. The fact is, however, that automating machines means sacrificing a very great deal of potential functionality. In order to automate a practical object, it is necessary to stereotype it in its function, thus making it more fragile. Far from having any intrinsic technical advantages, automatism always embodies the risk of arresting technical advance, for so long as an object has not been automated it remains susceptible of redesign, of self-transcendence through incorporation into a larger functional whole. When it becomes automatic, on the other hand, its function is fulfilled, certainly, but it is also hermetically sealed. Automatism amounts to a closing-off, to a sort of functional self-sufficiency which exiles man to the irresponsibility of a mere spectator. Contained within it is the dream of a dominated world, of a formally perfected technicity that serves an inert and dreamy humanity.[67]

While an object of relative technical sophistication might be able to perform the most extraordinary of tasks, tasks that perhaps were unthinkable even at the time when Baudrillard wrote the above, its functionality might be considered already known, and in some sense already fulfilled. One does not really use such an object, but rather allows it to perform its pre-ordained role. Of course there is more than a little pre-determination in the action of *The Way Things Go*;

as I have already suggested, objects do no more than they need to, no more than they are able. But while each object, whether a chair or a tyre, a ladder or a broom, does no more than it needs to in any particular situation, it can still adapt to different situations and perform a different role in each. The more automated object, on the other hand, may only work well if the particular circumstances in which it is placed are compatible with its functionality. (For example, for all its extraordinary sophistication, a modern mobile phone might, in most circumstances, have less actual functionality than a simple bowl, especially when it can't pick up a signal or its battery is flat.) By using such simple objects that are, for the most part, dependent on technology that is hundreds if not thousands of years old, Fischli and Weiss have allowed them to act in ways that are both familiar and completely unexpected.[68]

Baudrillard was not the first to question the lack of potentiality inherent in increased automatism, of course; perhaps one of the most important such critical enquiries, particularly in regard to our considerations of what might be deemed humorous, was made by Bergson in his essay 'Le Rire' ('Laughter', 1900). Bergson valued that which was spontaneous over that which was mechanical, and believed that life, as an *élan vital*, could not be understood through recourse to the strictures of reason. For him, it is intuition alone that possesses the flexibility to respond to the changing situations in which we find ourselves. Given the dangers that he foresaw in the increasing mechanisation of life and the consequent diminution of individuality, it might seem a little surprising that Bergson used his concerns to develop a theory of comedy, albeit one that would contribute to his broader philosophy of vitalism. Although he insists that 'it would be idle to attempt to derive every comic effect from one simple formula', he does admit that such a formula 'exists well enough in a certain sense', and it is not long before he describes comedy, rather simply, as '[s]omething mechanical encrusted on the living'.[69] By this Bergson does not necessarily mean anything so literal as a person acting like a machine — although the third of the three 'laws' he develops from this fundamental insight is the rather more general 'We laugh every time a person gives us the impression of being a thing'— but rather refers to some subtler forms of replacement, such as the substitution of the artificial for the natural, or the foregrounding of the physical when our attention should be turned to loftier matters.[70] It is perhaps obvious that these are simple examples of incongruity of the types explored earlier, and particular instances are easily found within *The Way Things Go*, as well as in Fischli and Weiss's practice more generally.

What Bergson's three laws share among themselves, as well as with other observations made within his essay, is the absorption of automatism within life — indeed, of its imitation of life — and the degree of rigidity that ensues, especially when compared to the mobility of that which is alive. Of course, for the philosopher of the *élan vital*, the body was considered the very example of suppleness, 'the ever-alert activity of a principle always at work', but this is not really the case, regardless of how much we would like it to be so.[71] As he points out:

When we see only gracefulness and suppleness in the living body, it is because we disregard in it the elements of weight, or resistance, and, in a word, of matter; we forget its materiality and think only of its vitality, a vitality which we regard as derived from the very principle of intellectual and moral life. Let us suppose, however, that our attention is drawn to the material side of the body; that, so far from sharing in the lightness and subtlety of the principle with which it is animated, the body is no more in our eyes than a heavy and cumbersome vesture, a kind of irksome ballast which holds down to earth a soul eager to rise aloft.[72]

When, a little further on, Bergson describes our experience of life as 'on the one hand, the moral personality with its intelligently varied energy, and, on the other, the stupidly monotonous body, perpetually obstructing everything with its machine-like obstinacy',[73] I think we can begin to see the source of much of the humour of *The Way Things Go*, and indeed of *Equilibres*. What these works share is an attempt to arrive at a state of, if not grace, then gracefulness, and at times I would argue that this is achieved, albeit temporarily. However, among the crashes and collapses, fallings and failings, we cannot escape the single-minded clumsiness of the things themselves. Indeed, perhaps this is what makes those momentary states of gracefulness so wonderful when they do occur; as the subtitle to *Equilibres* states: *Am schönsten ist das*

Gleichgewicht, kurz bevor's zusammenbricht (*Balance is most beautiful just before it collapses*).[74]

I shall return to this state of gracefulness shortly, but I want to consider further the contrary quality of the comic that, as Bergson remarks, 'partakes rather of the unsprightly than of the unsightly, of *rigidness* rather than of *ugliness*'.[75] The lack of flexibility of which he writes does not necessarily refer to the physical body – although obviously some of the most famous examples of humour, such as slapstick, rely on such awkwardness – but to a certain fixity of mind, whereby the observation of a code, or the repetition of a habit, becomes of the utmost importance, to the detriment of all else, even that which perhaps should have been best served by the actions. As Bergson observes, such a response can be found most clearly in the pedantry of the official, 'who performs his duty like a mere machine, or again in the unconsciousness that marks an administrative regulation working with inexorable fatality, and setting itself up for a law of nature'. By way of example, he quotes Doctor Bahis from Molière's *L'Amour médecin* (1665): 'It is better to die through following the rules than to recover through violating them'.[76] In suggesting that 'the mechanical application of rules here bring about a kind of professional automatism', Bergson considered such automatism the very antithesis of the *élan vital*, and could therefore be considered a form of death, a diminishing movement toward insensitive matter.[77] Earlier, the philosopher Félix Ravaisson had also considered the responses of a whole range of beings, from the inorganic world to human life, and suggested that the type of reaction changed, and became more sophisticated, as one went up the hierarchy of beings:

In the inorganic world, reaction is exactly equal to action, or rather, in this entirely external and superficial existence, action and reaction merge: they are one and the same act from two different points of view. In life, the action of the external world and the reaction of life itself become more and more different and appear to be more and more independent of each other. In vegetable life, they are more similar to each other and closely intertwined. Beginning at the first level of animal life, they move apart and differentiate themselves, and the more or less great agitations in space correspond to the imperceptible states of receptivity.[78]

As Jean Starobinski has recently commented, Ravaisson did not want to restrict action and reaction completely to the simultaneity so strongly asserted by others, including Kant, but instead 'uses the same term — "reaction" — to designate a phenomenon of the "mechanical world" and a *deferred* response given by man's "freest activity"'. It is not that the 'less and less immediate and necessary reaction' is delayed by 'an indifferent medium term such as the centre of opposite forces of the lever' — a reaction that is continuous to its cause, albeit somewhat delayed by the working through of the process — but rather that there is 'a centre that, by its own means, measures and disperses the energy'.[79]

I believe that we are moving toward a sense of why we find the objects — and their actions, their reactions —

in *The Way Things Go* so amusing. If it is the rigidity of that which is alive that makes us laugh — 'something mechanical encrusted on the living' — then the same is also true when the terms are reversed, *viz.* when something inanimate takes on the characteristics of the living. I would suggest that this is what occurs in *The Way Things Go*, and is one of the reasons for its humour. There are moments when, instead of acting automatically and with immediacy, simply falling or rolling, the objects seem to hesitate, as if reflecting on what it is they are about to do: the tyre resting among the burning newspapers before moving on, and resting again before rolling on once more; the can being filled with water before sliding down the orange slope; the lazy unfolding of the inflatable bed, like an arm stretching during a yawn. Of course, this is not always the case, and often the objects act exactly as we would expect, but there are occasions enough when the supposed symmetry of classical causality — 'to every action there is always opposed an equal reaction', in the famous formulation of Newton's third law of motion — does not occur, and the object falters, or fails to respond for some time, or seems to respond disproportionately. The humour occurs, then, when we refuse, or are unable, to see these as nothing more than the playing out of physical forces — the overcoming of inertia, for example — and instead attribute human characteristics to them. Although this might seem little more than simple anthropomorphism, by sensing the emergence of life, and even a degree of self-awareness, from the debris of objects, we become aware of an incongruity, and in that moment, it makes us laugh.

In sensing a pause, we are made aware of an act occurring in time, and of the possibility that it might have occurred rather earlier, or somewhat later; furthermore, if we continue to deny that the object is reacting entirely to physical forces, but rather view it as choosing to act — and importantly, as choosing when to act — then we also introduce the notion of timing.

'What's the secret of comedy?'

'I don't kn...'

'T-Timing.'

The above may seem to be its own best counter-argument (I admit, it is better heard than read), but it is widely agreed that timing is of crucial importance to comedy. The timing may relate to many things, such as when the joke is told, for example. It might be too soon, as in the case of 'sick' jokes, when it is felt that the tragedy to which it refers is too recent; or it might be too late, when the witty riposte does not come until one is leaving the situation in which it should have been made — *l'esprit d'escalier*, in Diderot's fine phrase. More often, of course, the timing in question lies in the telling of the joke itself, rather than the 'when' of the telling. Sometimes it is in the discrepancy between the setup and the punch-line, perhaps most famously in 'The Aristocrats' joke, where the humour resides almost entirely in how drawn-out is its telling (and yes, how filthy too); this is made obvious by the fact that the punch-line, which is normally hidden, is in fact the joke's name. Perhaps more often timing is thought of as the pause, the beat, before the punch-line is given, thereby raising the expectation of a laugh, and in delaying it, making it all the more welcome. (As the comedian Arnold Brown explained, 'There's a tradition in Jewish comedy for self-deprecation — but I'm not very good at it.') What both examples share, the digression and the pause, is the experience of two different temporal dimensions: *duration* and the *instant*.[80] As Simon Critchley puts it:

In being told a joke, we undergo a particular expression of duration through repetition and digression, of time literally being stretched out like an elastic band. We know that the elastic will snap, we just do not know when, and we find this anticipation rather pleasurable. It snaps with the punch-line, which is a sudden acceleration of time, where the digressive stretching of the joke suddenly contracts into a heightened experience of the instant.[81]

The Way Things Go is full of these shifts in time between the slow and the quick, the calm and the catastrophic, which is why it makes us laugh so. We watch expectantly, excitedly, as the kettle boils — has such an event ever prompted such intensity before? — before it screams at speed across the floor; or the expectation may lead to almost nothing, like the plastic cup that scrapes arcs back and forth across the width of an angled orange board, nearly slipping off the sides, but slowly sliding down the slope, until... it falls off the end, as when Kant talks of laughter as 'an affection arising from the strained expectation being suddenly reduced to nothing'.[82] And what of the fuse that flames brightly along the floor and up the bent-back blade of a saw, which supports and then releases it — *pyung* — flinging the flame through the air to light a ball of paper at the top of a pole some distance away? This scene is almost the perfect joke: anticipation, timing, physical slapstick and a punch-line that is not only delivered by the setup but actually is the setup, the payoff hidden within and smuggled across before our eyes.

I would go further and say that *The Way Things Go* is a master class in comic delivery, almost a compendium of techniques used by great comedians. At times, the scenes possess the logical absurdity of Tommy Cooper: 'So I got home, and the phone was ringing. I picked it up and said, "Who's speaking please?" And a voice said, "You are."';[83] at others, the chaotic clattering and collision of objects are reminiscent of Steven Wright:

Under my bed I have a shoe-box full of telephone rings. Whenever I get lonely I open it up just a bit and I get a call. One time I dropped the box all over the floor and the phone wouldn't stop ringing, so I had it disconnected. I bought a new phone though. I didn't have much money so I had to buy an irregular phone — it had no number 5 on it. I saw a close friend of mine the other day... He said, 'Steven, why haven't you called me?' I said, 'I can't call everyone I want. My new phone has no 5 on it.' He said, 'How long have you had it?' I said, 'I don't know... My calendar has no 7s on it.'[84]

Indeed, it would be interesting to learn how certain 'takes' in *The Way Things Go* were chosen from the numerous shots that must have been made of each scene; most of them are relatively short. I suspect that they were chosen not simply because the objects 'worked' —they 'lit' or 'hit' the things that they were supposed to — but rather because of *how* they worked, that they *delivered*.

Perhaps it is here that I should, however reluctantly, mention 'The Cog', the Honda Accord advertisement from 2003 that, shall we say, shares certain similarities with *The Way Things Go*.[85] The advertisement begins when a transmission bearing rolls into a synchro hub, thereby setting in motion a chain reaction using only parts from an Accord; in one rather memorable sequence — memorable in that it is reminiscent of something else — a series of weighted wheels rolls up an incline, each nudging the next to roll upward in turn. Two minutes and one cleverly hidden cut later, it all ends when a car rolls off a balanced trailer and Garrison Keillor intones in voice-over: 'Isn't it nice... when things just... *work*?'[86]

The advertisement differs most from Fischli and Weiss's film in what it lacks: it has none of the uncertainty of its predecessor, no sense of self-awareness, no sense at all that it wouldn't 'just work'. Of course, as the advertisement is for a car, one would hardly expect to see technology being portrayed as temperamental; it would not do to imply that the car might or might not start, much less that it might or might not stop.

Instead, everything works as it should, automatically, sometimes even invisibly, with no pause, no hesitation. And no joy. It might well be 'nice when things just work', if that is all that we want from things or the world in which we find them, but what if such a need is seen as being somewhat impoverished, the single vision of the mechanist against the four-fold vision of the artist?[87]

One can perhaps see this fundamental difference between the advertisement and the film most clearly in how both end. For the advertisement, the end is all, and everything that has preceded it was instrumental in bringing it to this conclusion; the car rolls down the trailer ramp (and somehow appears to brake) while a banner unfurls to the appropriately bragging soundtrack of The Sugarhill Gang. *Ta-Daa!* Conversely, *The Way Things Go* does not really seem to end at all, but rather dissolves in mist, from which one expects it to emerge at any moment. In that sense, it could have finished five minutes earlier, or continued for another 15, or even indefinitely, without ever coming to a sense of being complete.

While it is undoubtedly the result of an extraordinary amount of effort, both physical and conceptual, *The Way Things Go* possesses a 'purposeless purposiveness', to use Kant's term, that is completely inconceivable to the instrumental rationality of the advertisement, and that offers the possibility of something almost redemptive. If one must, one can admire the technical achievement of the advertisement, but I would suggest that this is somewhat irrelevant to our considerations; indeed, it is interesting that many people assume that the advertisement was made using CGI, an observation that, tellingly, seems to have been taken as a compliment by those involved in its making. It is clear that *The Way Things Go* does not depend on such technical perfection; we can clearly see how it was made, and where the cuts are, but that does not detract from the work at all. Indeed, it would seem to enhance it in some way, showing us that it is part of an ongoing process of creation *in which we too are involved*, rather than an automatic procedure of which we are no part. The film allows us an ongoing imagining of other forms of experience, and the advertisement finishes by asking us to look at a car and a flag; in taking itself so seriously, perhaps it doesn't need us to do so.[88]

In most of my discussions of jokes and actions within *The Way Things Go*, the examples possessed what Koestler referred to as 'a single point of culmination': tension is produced within a situation before being discharged, often through laughter, at a particular point.[89] However, there are many situations that are rather more complex, or more sustained, than such a singular event, and that are not resolved quite so simply. I think this is actually true for *The Way Things Go* as a whole, rather than for the isolated scenes within it. Certainly, many of these scenes are funny, their humour produced, perhaps, by a combination of absurd incongruity and the release of nervous energy that may be comparable to the release of kinetic energy within the film itself.[90] However, our response, in the main, is one of quiet amusement, of the smile rather than the laugh. In considering the relationship between these two responses, Critchley has pointed out that:

In many languages, smiling is a diminutive of laughter. In Latin, one distinguishes ridere *from* subridere, *laughter from sub- or under-laughter. The same is true in French and Italian:* rire *and* sourire, ridere *and* sorridere. *In German, one has the distinction between* das Lachen *and* das Lächlen, *or 'little laughter'. This is also present in Swedish* [...] *and elsewhere.*[91]

I would, however, like to make another etymological connection here, with a notion that I believe is of fundamental importance to the practice of Fischli and Weiss: *wonder*. After asking what words the 'medieval and early modern Europeans use for the modern English "wonder" and "wonders"', historians Lorraine Daston and Katharine Park answer: 'In Latin, the emotion itself was called *admiratio* and the objects, *mirabilia*, *miracula*, or occasionally *ammiranda*. These terms, like the verb *miror* and the adjective *mirus*, seem to have their roots in an Indo-European word for "smile".' Indeed, they remark that the 'ties between wonder and smiling persisted in the romance languages (*merveille* in French, *meraviglia* in Italian, *marvel* in English from ca.1300)'.[92] Perhaps it is this echo of meaning that plays across our faces when we visit an exhibition by Fischli and Weiss, watch one of their films, look at their works, read one of their books; the smile that we cannot help but give, even when we are not especially amused. It is a smile of wonder.

This smile is not ours alone, but sits with quiet benevolence on the faces of the artists too, and has done so since the very beginning of their collaboration. Just as one can hear the smile in the voice of someone talking over the phone, so one can see it in Fischli and Weiss's artworks. Just look at *At the Carpet Shop* from the *Sausage Series* once more. There is the smile of humour here, certainly, the amusement generated by the incongruity, the absurdity of making such a scene with such materials; but more than this, there is the smile of wonder too, that not only can one make such a scene in this way, but that one can make it *so well*. The same is true for the photographed assemblages in *Equilibres*, and of course for *The Way Things Go*. One might attempt something 'for a laugh', and humour can thereby arise even in failure; however, one can produce wonder *only* if one succeeds. Just as with the consideration of comic delivery in *The Way Things Go*, I believe that wonder – and its related, though contested, notion of curiosity – can be found in a great diversity throughout the practice of Fischli and Weiss, and not simply in the examples briefly mentioned. Indeed, I would suggest that these ideas provide the subject matter as well as the impetus for much of their work, and might even be considered as fundamental to it.

As Daston and Park have meticulously shown, what we understand by wonder and curiosity has undergone enormous shifts throughout the history of ideas, and both concepts have been praised, contested and dismissed by philosophers, theologians and scientists alike. Plato suggested that philosophy had no other origin, and Aristotle, similarly, remarked that 'It is owing to their wonder that men both now begin and at first began to philosophise.'[93] But this seeking of knowledge that Aristotle and his Latin commentators had claimed as natural to humanity had little to do with what was then (and later) understood by curiosity; if, later, 'for medieval natural philosophers wonder was a necessary if uncomfortable (and therefore ideally short-lived) realisation of ignorance', then 'curiosity was the morally ambiguous desire to know that which did not concern one, be it the secrets of nature or of one's neighbours'.[94] Daston and Park cite St. Augustine, perhaps the most influential critic of curiosity, as stating it was at best 'perverted and futile; and at worst it was a distraction from God and Salvation'. Curiosity was the cause of undue pride and opposed to the wonder of God, because it seemed ultimately more interested in its own importance as investigation, rather than in the importance of that which was *under* investigation; such was Augustine's complaint against the astronomers, whom he considered to be suffering 'from an excess of curiosity and a deficiency of awe'.[95]

The relationship between an elevated sense of wonder and a morbid curiosity changed markedly over the coming centuries, however, and by the middle of the seventeenth century the terms became allied, with wonder acting as an impetus to enquiry. According to Daston and Park, Descartes considered it to be the first of the passions, 'a sudden surprise of the soul which makes it tend to consider attentively those objects which seem to it rare and extraordinary', while Francis Bacon included a 'history of marvels' in his proposed reform of natural philosophy.[96] It is clear, however, that wonder was becoming merely the starting point for what was increasingly considered to be more important: the acts of investigation driven by sustained, indeed relentless, curiosity. Furthermore, it was thought that wonder in excess – that is, stupefying astonishment – might even arrest this important search for knowledge. Descartes himself thought astonishment 'makes the whole body [and mind] remain immobile like a statue [...] and therefore cannot acquire any more particular knowledge', while Bacon scorned the natural philosophers whose enquiries 'ever breaketh off in wondering and not in knowing'.[97] These concerns grew ever stronger, and by the middle of the eighteenth century wonder and curiosity were once again opposed to one another, although now their respective statuses were the opposite of those they'd held in the age of Augustine. Now, '[n]oble curiosity worked hard and shunned enticing novelties; vulgar wonder wallowed in the pleasures of novelty and obstinately refused to remedy the ignorance that aroused it.'[98] Curiosity had become earnest application; wonder little more than gaudy spectacle.[99]

Our understanding of these terms has changed further in the past 250 years or so, and even if we wished to situate the work of Fischli and Weiss in relation to a particular historical understanding – a foolhardy task in any case – it would create certain problems. That is not to say, however, that certain of these ideas might not open up a space in which we might think further about these works; indeed, one might even argue that these works allow us the opportunity to question our own contemporary notions of wonder and curiosity, and allow us to experience a new sense of both.[100] With that said, I would suggest that it is the very simplicity of their works, if simplicity is the right word for works of such intellectual and emotional complexity, that allows for such a reconsideration of these two terms. The installation for the 1995 Venice Biennale, for example — 32 videos in total, each three hours long — might suggest a certain sense of the grandiose, but once one begins to watch the videos themselves — of cats drinking milk, or a trip to the dentist or a night-club — this grandiosity disappears completely. There is certainly little attempt made here to follow Robert Hooke's advice:

[A]*n Observer should endeavour to look upon such Experiments and Observations that are more common, and to which he has been more accustom'd, as if they were the greatest Rarity, and to imagine himself a Person of some other Country or Calling, that he had never heard of, or seen the like before.*[101]

In *Visible World*, a work that is in many ways the complement of the Venice videos, we do indeed find things of the 'greatest Rarity' — the Egyptian pyramids, for example, or the Ryōan-ji Zen garden in Kyoto or a glacier — and yet each is portrayed with the utmost familiarity; and there are, indeed, more familiar street scenes, even if the streets are on the other side of the world from the Swiss hills. These works sit uneasily between the spectacle of the advertising image and the self-consciousness of the 'critical' image, or perhaps those image types are now made to sit uneasily on either side of *Visible World*'s calm assuredness. As David Weiss recently remarked:

And the 'critical' image doesn't explain the fascination of the Pyramids in any case. There is a reason why the Pyramids are famous. When you go there, no matter how many photographs you've seen of them before, you realise that the Pyramids are unique, and that you don't understand them. There is a reason why these sites are powerful; there's a reason why the waves in the sea are emotionally attractive, and we wanted to explore these images, knowing that they were in some ways forbidden fruits.[102]

I think that what the artists are doing here — an exploration of wonder and curiosity, the uncommon and the familiar — is something similar to that which Martin Heidegger explored in a series of lectures given at the University of Freiburg in 1937–38, and later published under the title *Basic Questions of Philosophy: Selected 'Problems' of Logic*. Although acknowledging that the Greeks recognised wonder as the 'beginning' of philosophy, Heidegger goes on to argue not only that we misunderstand what was meant by such a term, and therefore confuse it with curiosity, but also that this original sense of wonder, and therefore philosophy itself, is now lost to us. As he remarks in a later essay, what is '[m]ost thought-provoking is that we are still not thinking — not even yet'.[103]

In the first essay, Heidegger explores three terms that he believes are incorrectly viewed as synonymous with wonder – amazement, admiration and astonishment – but he is also keen to show how different they are from what must have originally been meant by the concept.

In many ways, his criticisms are similar to the concerns raised by philosophers such as Descartes and Bacon, among others, although perhaps somewhat intensified; whereas his predecessors still saw value in wonder and were wary of its distortion through excess and debasement, for Heidegger these corrupted versions are not only all that are available to us, but are also all that we, the not-Greeks, can ever really know. And so, while we might be amazed by a particular object or situation, if we become familiar with it, then our sense of amazement, and with it our sense of wonder, is lost. It is this loss that compels us in the pursuit for novelty, which 'makes the search for every new thing of this kind more ardent'.[104] For Heidegger, even the admiration of a situation or person is an act of lowering the status of the object of that admiration, for 'he subordinates himself to the viewpoint and to the norms of his admirer'.[105] Similarly, the sense of wonder commonly understood to coincide with admiration is particularly fragile; as soon as the admiration is gone (when the achievement of the person admired is bettered, perhaps), the wonder goes too. Even astonishment – that is, an encounter with that which is truly awesome, that which can be neither understood nor explained – demands that the object of astonishment be 'extraordinary', and as such, be subject to a law of diminishing returns. If what was sublime became the norm, it would no longer be considered sublime.

While we might, in our lazy way with words, refer to the work of Fischli and Weiss as 'amazing' or 'astonishing' (and I know that I have), perhaps we are thereby doing it a disservice, albeit an unintentional one. Perhaps a work like *The Way Things Go* is attempting something more extraordinary, something thought impossible by Heidegger himself: to approach what he considered to be the 'wondrous'. In defining the term, Heidegger writes that it is 'for us in the first place something that stands out and therefore is remarkable; for the most part it also has the character of the exceptional, unexpected, surprising, and therefore exciting. A better name for this would be the curious or the marvellous'.[106] As Brad Stone has remarked in his commentary on the lectures of Heidegger:

Unlike curiosity, which presupposes that there is a difference between the usual and the unusual (the extraordinary), wonder is an attunement in which one finds even the usual to be extraordinary. The wondrous is not the extraordinary; instead, it is the unusualness of what is usual. As Heidegger states, '[i]*n wonder* [...] *everything becomes the most unusual.* [...] *Everything in what is most usual (beings) becomes in wonder the most unusual in this one respect: that it is what it is.'* [...] *The extraordinary is right under our noses; what is wondrous is that beings 'be'.*[107]

I think that this is perhaps as succinct and accurate a summation of the practice of Fischli and Weiss as

I have found. In denying a distinction between the usual and the unusual, between the ordinary and the extraordinary, wonder allows no escape into, or retreat from, the unusualness of usual beings. As Stone points out, if everything is unusual, then there is no 'usual' to which we can return once we tire of the unusual, nor is there a 'usual' for us to flee in our pursuit of curiosity. He continues:

Once in this attunement, there is no way to overcome or to avoid wonder; one must think. *Wonder shows that the usual and the unusual are two sides of the same coin: that beings 'be', whether we take them for granted as merely being 'usual', or by philosophically thinking of them in their extraordinariness. Wonder is 'between' the usual and the unusual insofar as it is in wonder that the usual is unusual, and vice-versa.*[108]

I would argue that Fischli and Weiss have achieved this 'attunement', and are thereby able to feel wonder, and to allow us a sense of what it might feel like too. We can sense it in a sculpture like *Son et lumière* (1990), for example, which incorporates a rotating cake stand that the artists spotted in a shop window in Brazil – how mundane, how exotic – around which is placed a rim of masking tape and on which is placed a cheap plastic tumbler, one of those that imitate cut crystal. This little assembly is placed on a plinth, near the wall, and in front of it, on the plinth, is a small torch, its light shining straight onto and through the tumbler. And of course, as the turntable turns and the tumbler tumbles, arcs of light, green or red, flitter across the wall, dissolving, diving, emerging, soaring. 'Utterly simple and utterly compelling.'[109] It is astonishing, yes, and yet no matter how many times one sees it, and no matter for how long one looks at it, it remains this. It is admirable, yes, and yet it is not diminished by being so – the lowliness of its materials allows no possibility of a fall. It is amazing, yes, and yet it does not stop being so once explained, as no explanation is necessary; we can see exactly how it works, and yet we have no idea how it works. This is perhaps as close to an experience of aesthetic wonder as it is possible to get.

But of course, this was not the first work by Fischli and Weiss of which this could be said; just a few years earlier, *The Way Things Go* achieved exactly the same thing, and may be their most wondrous work of all. While this is something that I've only become conscious of in the writing of this book, it is something that I've *known* since that first afternoon at the ICA so long ago, something that all of us there knew, and it was this that brought us to our feet in applause. A sense of wonder that spilled earlier from the TV screen produced a curiosity that brought us to London to learn more, to see more, and in so doing allowed us to experience a sense of the wondrous that has yet to dull. It is a wonder that refuses to be diminished, no matter how familiar the film has become, no matter that I may now actually anticipate certain actions; rather, is reinvigorated by each viewing, recharged by our presence, ignited by our smile. It is a film of simple means and complex ends, a film that allows another way of being in the world, a way in which meaning can emerge, and continue to emerge; a film that makes one laugh, and smile, and a film that might just be about everything, and not just everything there is, but everything there has been and might well be. Has there ever been, will there ever be, a better artists' film? I wonder.

1
Tony Wilson died on 10 August 2007, during the proof stage of this book. Like many people, I owe a great deal to Wilson not only for making me aware of particular musicians (mainly) or artists about whom I might not otherwise have heard, but also for the manner in which he did so. Watching his TV programmes, we had the sense that he was acknowledging our intelligence, that we deserved something this good, and that we might do something as good in our turn. As Mark Fisher has written in his blog entry (24 August 2007):

It was to Wilson's credit that he was never ashamed of his background; instead of indulging in tedious guilt trips or pop(ul)ist gestures, he used what resources he had to support the production of popular art works that anyone could buy. Wilson might have been an inveterate show-off, but the audience he courted were working class youth. He might have wanted to beguile and entrance them, to impress them with his learning and his eloquence, but better that – far better that – than pretending to be more stupid than you are, as more or less every educated person is required to do to get on in Old Media today...

See http://k-punk.abstractdynamics.org
With thanks to Mark for bringing this to my attention.

2
Laurence Sterne, *The Life and Opinions of Tristram Shandy, Gentleman*, London: Penguin Books, 1997, p.58. Originally published in serial form, London: Ann Ward (vol.1–2), Dodsley (vol.3–4), Becket and DeHondt (vol.5–9), 1759–67.

3
Aloïs Riegl, *Historical Grammar of the Visual Arts* (trans. Jacqueline E. Jung), New York: Zone Books, 2004, p.385. Of course this is not to single out Riegl, one of the greatest writers on art, for particular criticism; the point I hope to make is more general, and one of historic shifts rather than individual failings.

4
Pliny the Younger, *Natural History* (XXXVI, 37), ca.100 CE.

5
This was Laocöon's disbelieving response upon hearing the explanation given by Sinon, a captured Achaean, for the Wooden Horse found deserted on the plains outside Troy. Even after having undergone disfiguring torture, Sinon insisted that it was nothing more than an offering to placate the goddess Athena; of course, as the person responsible for releasing the soldiers from the Horse once it had been brought within the city walls, and for signalling the return of the Achaean army in order to attack Troy, Sinon knew that the Horse was something else entirely. Laocoön, as quoted by Quintus Smyrnaeus, *The Fall of Troy* (XII, 390), ca.400 CE.

6
Peter Fischli quoted in 'The Odd Couple' (interview with Jörg Heiser), *frieze*, October 2006, p.205.

7
Michel Leiris, *Roussel & Co*, Paris: Fata Morgana/Fayard, 1998, pp.175–76; quoted in Mark Ford, *Raymond Roussel and the Republic of Dreams*, London: Faber and Faber, 2000, p.30. I am indebted to Ford's book, which I recommend to those interested not only in Roussel's work, but also in the development of the avant-garde in the twentieth century.

8
Marcel Duchamp, from an interview with James Johnson Sweeney, *The Bulletin of The Museum of Modern Art*, vol.XIII nos.4–5, 1946, pp.19–21; reprinted in Michel Sanouillet and Elmer Peterson (eds.), *The Writings of Marcel Duchamp*, New York: Da Capo Press, 1973, p.126. Alain Robbe-Grillet, 'Enigmes et transparence chez Raymond Roussel' (1963) (trans. Barbara Wright as 'Riddles and Transparencies in Raymond Roussel'), in Alistair Brotchie *et al.* (eds.), *Atlas Anthology 4: Raymond Roussel – Life, Death, and Works*, London: Atlas Press, 1987. Michel Foucault, *Death and the Labyrinth: The World of Raymond Roussel* (trans. Charles Ruas), London: Athlone Press, 1987.

9
Raymond Roussel, *How I Wrote Certain of My Books* (trans. Trevor Winkfield), Boston, Mass.: Exact Change, 1995, p.6.

10
Raymond Roussel, *Impressions of Africa* (trans. Lindy Foord and Rayner Heppenstall), Berkeley: University of California Press, 1967; quoted in André Breton, *Anthology of Black Humor* (trans. Mark Polizzotti), San Francisco: City Lights Books, 1997, pp.230–33.

11
Indeed, these correspondences may strike one as an example of *apophrades*, the sixth revisionary ratio established by Harold Bloom in his appropriately influential book, *The Anxiety of Influence* (1973). Bloom defines his term thus: '*Apophrades*, or the return of the dead; I take the word from the Athenian dismal or unlucky days upon which the dead returned to reinhabit the houses in which they had lived. The later poet, in his own final phase, already burdened by an imaginative solitude that is almost a solipsism, holds his own poem so open again to the precursor's work that at first we might believe the wheel has come full circle, and that we are back in the latter poet's flooded apprenticeship, before his strength began to assert itself in the revisionary ratios. But the poem is now *held* open to the precursor, where once it *was* open, and the uncanny effect is that the new poem's achievement makes it seem to us, not as though the precursor were writing it, but as though the later poet himself had written the precursor's

characteristic work.' Harold Bloom, *The Anxiety of Influence*, Oxford and New York: Oxford University Press, 1997, pp.15–16. This may suggest too direct and knowing a relationship between Fischli and Weiss's work and Roussel's which preceded it, although I think the uncanny, no doubt unconscious sense that they share is well-described here.

12
R. Roussel, *How I Wrote Certain of My Books*, *op. cit.*, p.16.

13
Peter Fischli quoted in 'Interview: Beate Söntgen in Conversation with Peter Fischli and David Weiss', in Robert Fleck *et al.*, *Peter Fischli/ David Weiss*, London: Phaidon Press, 2005, p.23.

14
Søren Kierkegaard, *Either/Or: A Fragment of Life* (trans. Alistair Hannay), Harmondsworth: Penguin Books, 1992, p.227.

15
Henri Focillon, *The Life of Forms in Art* (trans. Charles B. Hogan and George Kubler), New York: Zone Books, 1989, p.41.

16
Ibid., p.137.

17
Patrick Frey, 'The Successful Failure', in *Peter Fischli David Weiss*, Cambridge, Mass.: The MIT List Visual Arts Center, 1987, pp.20–21.

18
David Weiss, quoted in 'The Odd Couple', *op. cit.*, pp.202–05.

19
Franz Reuleaux, *Cinématique: Principes fondamentaux d'une théorie générale des machines* (1875, trans. 1877); quoted by Jean-François Lyotard in 'Considerations on Certain Partition-Walls as the Potentially Bachelor Elements of a Few Simple Machines', in Jean Clair and Harald Szeemann (eds.), *Le Macchine Celibi/The Bachelor Machines*, Venice: Alfieri, 1975, p.98.

20
The largest extant collection of these can be found at Cornell University; Cornell's first president, Andrew Dickson White, acquired a collection of 266 Reuleaux models for the university in 1882, and 220 of these are still owned by the Sibley School of Mechanical and Aerospace Engineering. They are still used in the teaching of design, dynamics, robotics, art and architecture, as well as in historical research. See http://kmoddl.library.cornell.edu/rx_collection.php

21
One might also think of the American cartoonist Rube Goldberg (1883–1970), whose name in his native country has, like Heath Robinson's in the United Kingdom, become synonymous with unnecessarily elaborate devices which perform the most basic of tasks. For those of us brought up on British TV in the late 1970s, the mechanisms created or overseen by Wilf Lunn on *Vision On* (BBC1, 1964–77) and Prof. Heinz Wolff on *The Great Egg Race* (BBC1, 1978–86) might also be brought to mind.

22
Much of the following information on Taylor was taken from Robert Kanigel's somewhat laudatory biography *The One Best Way: Frederick Winslow Taylor and the Enigma of Efficiency*, London: Little, Brown and Company, 1997.

23
Yevgeny Zamyatin, *We* (trans. Bernard Guilbert Guerney), Harmondsworth: Penguin Books, 1972, p.47.

24
R. Kanigel, *The One Best Way*, *op. cit.*, p.419.

25
A poem included in a letter by William Blake to his great patron Thomas Butts famously concludes: 'May God us keep/From single vision and Newton's sleep!' As Blake had a few lines previously stated, 'Now I a fourfold vision see', his opinion of the scientist's relative impoverishment could scarcely be clearer. 'To Thomas Butts' in *The Selected Poems of William Blake*, Ware: Wordsworth Editions, 2000, pp.146–8.

26
Reprinted in M. Sanouillet and E. Peterson (eds.), *The Writings of Marcel Duchamp*, *op. cit.*, p.160.

27
See Jeffrey Weiss, *The Popular Culture of Modern Art: Picasso, Duchamp, and Avant-Gardism*, New Haven, Conn. and London: Yale University Press, 1994, pp.107–63, and in particular pp.127–28.

28
Linda Dalrymple Henderson, *Duchamp in Context: Science and Technology in the* Large Glass *and Related Works*, Princeton, N.J.: Princeton University Press, 1998.

29
See also the entry for 4 June 1964, 'Ephemerides on and about Marcel Duchamp and Rrose Sélavy', texts by Jennifer Gough-Cooper and Jacques Caumont, in Pontus Hulton (ed.), *Marcel Duchamp: Work and Life*, Cambridge, Mass.: MIT Press, 1993.

30
M. Ford, *Raymond Roussel and the Republic of Dreams*, *op. cit.*, p.18.

31
'There is no document of civilisation which is not at the same time a document of barbarism.' Walter Benjamin, 'Theses on the Philosophy of History', *Illuminations* (trans. Harry Zohn), London: Fontana Press, 1992, p.248. The '*Vertigo* effect' or 'dolly zoom' was developed by Irmin Roberts, and was perhaps first used by Alfred Hitchcock in the 1958 film that gives the move its name. This disorienting effect was created by zooming the camera lens into a subject while simultaneously moving the camera away from the subject; the relative size of the subject within the image frame remains the same, but the perspective changes (in this case, a flattening sense of space), creating an effect that is difficult to locate and therefore extremely unsettling. Of course, the opposite movements can also be made, moving the camera toward the subject while simultaneously zooming out, an effect used most notably in Steven Spielberg's *Jaws* (1975) and much imitated since.

32
Archytas, as cited by Simplicius, in *Aristotelis Categorias Commentarium*; quoted in Edward S. Casey, *Getting Back Into Place: Toward a Renewed Understanding of the Place-World*, Bloomington and Indianapolis, Ind.: Indiana University Press, 1993, p.14.

33
Edward S. Casey, *The Fate of Place*, Berkeley and Los Angeles: University of California Press, 1998, p.8.

34
Ibid., p.12.

35
H. Focillon, *The Life of Forms in Art*, *op. cit.*, p.65.

36
E.S. Casey, *The Fate of Place*, *op. cit.*, p.18.

37
Ibid., p.19.

38
Henri Bergson, *Creative Evolution* (trans. Arthur Mitchell), Mineola, N.Y.: Dover Publications, 1998, p.341.

39
Ibid., p.340. One might also be reminded of a story which the great Italian writer Italo Calvino had planned to relate in a lecture on 'Quickness' at

Harvard in 1985, although his death on 19 September of that year prevented its telling; it concerned the great Chinese philosopher Chuang-Tzu. 'Among Chuang-Tzu's many skills he was an expert draftsman. The king asked him to draw a crab, Chuang-Tzu replied that he needed five years, a country house, and 12 servants. Five years later the drawing was still not begun. "I need another five years," said Chuang-Tzu. The king granted them. At the end of these ten years, Chuang-Tzu took up his brush and, in an instant, with a single stroke, he drew a crab, the most perfect crab ever seen.' Italo Calvino, 'Quickness', *Six Memos for the Next Millennium* (trans. Patrick Creagh), London: Jonathan Cape, 1992, p.54.

40
Such an attitude can even be found in the text on the back of the DVD case of *The Way Things Go*, which informs us that: 'Inside a warehouse, a precarious structure 70—100 feet long was constructed from various items.' Not only is this a literal spatialisation of the film, for all its vagueness, but it is hardly accurate; as we shall see, the film is made up of numerous shots, and it is extremely unlikely that the structure ever existed in its entirety at any one time, although this was no doubt as dependent on the amount of space available as on the (undoubted) difficulty in engineering a single take.

41
H. Bergson, *Creative Evolution*, *op. cit.*, pp.9—10.

42
There are a couple of other occasions, both just before and just after the kettles sequence, where what look like sugar cubes are piled one on top of another as a support which then gives way, allowing that which is above it to fall. Although these have been described as sugar cubes, and in the context of our discussion on Bergson it would be nice if they were, I suspect by their sound and the way they react that they might instead be small cubes of expanded polystyrene being dissolved by some form of solvent, something which occurs just before and just after these events, and near the very end of the film as well.

43
See Mary McAllester Jones (ed.), *Gaston Bachelard: Subversive Humanist*, Madison, Wis.: University of Wisconsin Press, 1991.

44
Gaston Bachelard, from *L'Intuition de l'instant*; quoted in *ibid.*, p.29. Also cited in Pamela M. Lee, *Chronophobia: On Time in the Art of the 1960s*, Cambridge, Mass. and London: The MIT Press, 2004, pp.123—24. Lee also discusses Bachelard's criticism of Bergson's concept of duration.

45
R. Fleck, 'Adventures Close to Home', in *Peter Fischli/David Weiss*, *op. cit.*, p.60. (Emphasis mine.)

46
Arthur C. Danto, 'The Artist as Prime Mover: Thoughts on Peter Fischli and David Weiss's *The Way Things Go*', in *ibid.*, p.105. However, slightly earlier in the essay, Danto remarks that 'we're pretty sure we can see the places in which the hands of the artists have intervened, to make things go the way they are supposed to go'. (*Ibid.*, pp.104–05.) As such, while Danto acknowledges the artists' (often apparent) interventions and the fact that for the most part we ignore them, seeing instead 'with the eyes of faith', he then goes on to align the artists with Leibniz, and with his belief 'that there is a pre-established harmony between cause and effect, and that once the machinery is in motion, there is nothing left for God to do', against his opponent Samuel Clarke, who believed 'that nothing in the universe happens without the intervention of God'. Therefore, instead of seeing the title of this film as somehow supportive of a seventeenth-century notion of a well-designed and perfectly functioning universe, perhaps *The Way Things Go* better describes a universe of uncertainty and wonder, albeit one in which we are more clearly involved.

47
As such, while I am hesitant to disagree once more with a writer as eminent as Danto, I think it is a mistake to say that 'It is important to the success of the work that its means remain concealed' (*ibid.*, p.104). What Danto was unaware of at the time of writing his essay was that two three-hour videotapes had been recorded by Patrick Frey of the first attempts made in September 1985, an extract of which was projected alongside the finished film in Fischli and Weiss's recent touring exhibition in London, Paris, Zürich and Hamburg. While I would question the inclusion of this video, *Making Things Go*, alongside the film, this is more to do with the way in which it distracts the viewer rather than the fact that it reveals how things were done (it seems an uncharacteristic misstep, in my view). Indeed, as I shall discuss later, it is made perfectly clear in the film itself how it was made; Frey's video seems to be an answer to an unnecessary question.

48
Arthur C. Danto, 'Play/Things', in Elizabeth Armstrong (ed.), *Peter Fischli and David Weiss: In a Restless World*, Minneapolis, Minn.: Walker Art Center, 1996, p.105.

49
Mikhail Mikhailovich Bakhtin, 'Epic and Novel: Toward a Methodology for the Study of the Novel', in *The Dialogic Imagination* (trans. Caryl Emerson and Michael Holquist), Austin, Tx.: University of Texas Press, 1981, p.13.

50
Ibid., p.16.

51
Ibid., p.21.

52
Bruno Schulz, 'Tailor's Dummies', *The Street of Crocodiles & Sanatorium Under the Sign of the Hourglass* (trans. Celina Wieniewska), London: Picador, 1988, p.41.

53
M.M. Bakhtin, 'Epic and Novel', *op. cit.*, p.23.

54
A particularly wonderful example of this occurred on 5 December 2006, when the Bishop of Southwark, the Right Reverend Tom Butler, is alleged to have become drunk after consuming a quantity of Portuguese red wine at the Irish Embassy's Christmas party. He appeared at a church service the next day with a black eye and without his mitre, which did not fit his bruised and swollen head; he'd sustained the injuries the previous night when, as he remarked to the congregation, he 'had apparently been mugged'. However, it soon emerged that the Bishop had been seen climbing into the back of a parked Mercedes before winding down the window and throwing out a number of infant's toys. When confronted by the owner of the car and asked to explain himself, Butler is supposed to have replied, 'I'm the Bishop of Southwark. It's what I do.' See David Bishop, 'Drink Row Bishop Facing Calls to Quit', *The Observer*, 10 December 2006.

55
Thomas Hobbes, *Leviathan* (1651), part I, chapter 6; quoted in Noël Carroll, 'Horror and Humor', *The Journal of Aesthetics and Art Criticism*, vol.57 no.2, p.153. With thanks to Michael Newall for bringing this and other humour-related papers to my attention.

56
Francis Hutcheson, *Reflections on Laughter*, Glasgow, 1750; reprinted in John Morreall (ed.), *The Philosophy of Laughter and Humor*, New York: SUNY Press, 1987, p.32. This passage is also quoted in N. Carroll, 'Horror and Humor', *op. cit.*, p.153. Similarly, and far earlier, Marcus Tullius Cicero noted in *De Oratore* (55 BCE) that 'The most common kind of joke is that in which we expect one thing and another is said; here our own disappointed expectation makes us laugh.'

57
George Orwell, 'Boys' Weeklies', first published in *Horizon* no.3, London, 1940; reprinted in *Inside the Whale and Other Essays*, Harmondsworth: Penguin Books, 1981, pp.187–88.

58
Arthur Koestler, *The Act of Creation*, London: Picador, 1975, p.27.

59
Ibid., p.33.

60
Ibid., pp.32–33.

61
Ibid., p.35.

62
Ibid.

63
Ibid., p.36. Another good example of the intersection of different associative contexts is a joke, one of my favourites, told to me by Ceal Floyer, an artist whose work might often also be considered 'bisociative': 'A woman goes into a bar and asks the bartender for a *double entendre*. So he gives her one.'

64
Peter Fischli, in Claire Bishop and Mark Godfrey, 'Fischli and Weiss: Between Spectacular and Ordinary', *Flash Art*, November/December 2006, p.76.

65
A. Koestler, *The Act of Creation*, *op. cit.*, p.56.

66
In both cases, we watch the kettles for only about ten seconds each before their explosive acts, although the sense of anticipation – it is clear what will happen next – perhaps extends our perception of the time elapsed. Actually, the duration of the first episode might have been longer, but a swift cut just before the kettle bursts into action has shortened the wait, and perhaps maintained a tension that might otherwise have dissipated.

67
Jean Baudrillard, *The System of Objects* (trans. James Benedict), London: Verso, 1996, p.110.

68
I have written previously of the 'functional transcendence' of objects in the work of fellow Swiss artist Roman Signer, who similarly uses a basic vocabulary of forms – tables, chairs, balloons, bicycles, fireworks – to create works of formal simplicity and emotional complexity. And, like the work of Fischli and Weiss, it is also extremely funny. See 'Catastrophe Practice' in *Roman Signer*, Kilkenny: Butler Gallery, 2001. This essay also

formed the basis of an even shorter piece published to coincide with an exhibition by Signer in London – *Roman Signer*, London: Camden Arts Centre, 2001.

69
Henri Bergson, 'Laughter', in Wylie Sypher (ed.), *Comedy*, Baltimore and London: Johns Hopkins University Press, 1980, p.84.

70
Ibid., p.97; pp.85–92; pp.92–97.

71
Ibid., p.92.

72
Ibid.

73
Ibid., pp.78–79.

74
Peter Fischli and David Weiss, *Stiller Nachmittag*, New York and Cologne: Sonnabend Gallery and Monika Sprüth Galerie, 1985, n.p.

75
H. Bergson, 'Laughter', *op. cit.*, p.79.

76
Ibid., pp.90 and 95. A rather more contemporary example, and one in which the protagonist is following his own sense of 'what is right' against more widely accepted social norms, is Larry David in the TV series *Curb Your Enthusiasm*. Here it is funny, excruciatingly so, when David is unable to reflect for a moment that in a particular circumstance, it might be best *not* to respond, and he pursues each perceived flaw in the social fabric, actual or not, until it rests shredded in his hands. However, if we were to watch a machine acting rather more literally – tearing material for recycling, for example – then we would do so with neither amusement nor embarrassment.

77
This might be considered an echo of Kant's earlier theorem on inertia:

The inertia of matter is and signifies nothing but its lifelessness, as matter in itself. Life means the capacity of a substance to determine itself to act from an internal principle. [...] *Now, we know of no other internal principle of a substance to change its state but desire and no other internal activity whatever but thought, along with what depends upon such desire, namely, feelings of pleasure or displeasure and appetite as well. But these determining grounds and actions do not at all belong to the representations of the external senses and hence also not to the determinations of matter as matter. Therefore all matter as such is lifeless.*

Immanuel Kant, *Metaphysical Foundations of Natural Science* (1786), cited by Jean Starobinski in *Action and Reaction* (trans. Sophie Hawkes), New York: Zone Books, 2003, p.47.

78
Ibid., p.272.

79
Ibid., pp.273, 272. The French novelist Etienne Pivert de Senancour describes something similar in his *Rêveries sur la nature primitive de l'homme* (1799), where he writes of an 'organised being' that '[i]f its organisation is more complicated, it retains the imprint of past sensations; hence it has the ability to enact several different reactions; it deliberates, it exercises choice.' Quoted in *ibid.*, p.251. Of course, this introduces the complex notion of 'free will' into the discussion; it goes without saying that I have little choice but to put this to one side in the context of this essay.

80
See Simon Critchley, *On Humour*, London: Routledge, 2002, p.7.

81
Ibid.

82
I. Kant, *Critique of Judgement* (1790) (trans. J.C. Meredith), Oxford: Clarendon Press, 1952; quoted in John Lippitt, 'Humour', in David E. Cooper (ed.), *A Companion to Aesthetics*, Oxford: Blackwell, 1992, p.199.

83
Tommy Cooper's memorable one-line jokes, or Cooperisms as they have been called, benefited greatly from the comedian's wet-eyed, loose-jawed delivery, although many continue to be circulated online. Examples can be found at: http://www.guysports.com/humor/comedians/comedian_tommy_cooper.htm

84
A large number of Steven Wright jokes and one-liners are available online; a good selection can be found at http://growabrain.typepad.com/growabrain/comedians_steven_wright/index.html. See also the comedian's own website at http://www.stevenwright.com. Another favourite of mine seems to recall some of the titles to be found within Fischli and Weiss's *Equilibres*: 'I like to go to art museums and name the untitled paintings... *Boy with Pail... Kitten on Fire.*'

85
I have little interest here in discussing the legal relationship between this advertisement and *The Way Things Go*, or the disputed notions of influence, copying and intellectual property rights, and still less in considering its effectiveness as advertising. (Like many other people, I have a view on the relationship between the works, but suspect that counsel would advise that I keep my own counsel.) Indeed, it is with a certain regret that I am making any reference to the advertisement in this book at all, an act which in itself might be seen as cultural legitimisation; however, perhaps the criticisms that follow will illuminate what is so important in Fischli and Weiss's film, and what is absent in the advertisement. Further information on the advertisement is widely available online, although I don't think that the irony of the car's name has been commented upon. Perhaps those involved might like to look at another, later piece by Fischli and Weiss, *How To Work* (1991), a series of ten 'rules' which were produced as screen-print posters, as well as painted onto the side of a large office building in Zürich-Oerlikon. Rule seven, in particular, reads: 'Admit mistakes'.

86
Given the rather contentious nature of the advertisement, and the parodies that have been made of it, it is interesting to recall that Keillor was himself the subject of one of *The Simpsons*' more memorable parodies. In 'Marge on the Lam' (first screened 4 November 1993), the family is watching a telethon in which a humorist – obviously based upon Keillor – is reading out a monologue on the week's events in the small town of Badger Falls, and during which the studio audience laughs and applauds loudly. The Simpsons are not amused, however, and Bart suggests that there might be something wrong with their set. Homer then gets up and begins hitting it, shouting 'Stupid TV. Be more funny!' The comment is not inappropriate here.

87
See note 25, above.

88
That the advertisement lacks humour almost goes without saying, although perhaps it should be stated for the record: it does not smile, much less laugh, but smirks, rather smugly. Compare this with the parody (of the film? Of the advertisement?) made as a viral web advertisement for 118118.com, which at least possesses some of the absurdity and humour of Fischli and Weiss's original film. Needless to say, the agency behind 'The Cog' was not amused by its appropriation.

89
A. Koestler, *The Act of Creation*, *op. cit.*, p.37.

90
The theory of a discharge of nervous or psychical energy through laughter was developed by Freud and based upon an earlier, rather simpler, version proposed by Herbert Spencer. See Sigmund Freud, *Jokes and their Relation to the Unconscious* (trans. John Strachey), Harmondsworth: Penguin Books, 1976.

91
S. Critchley, On Humour, *op. cit.*, p.108.

92
Lorraine Daston and Katharine Park, *Wonders and the Order of Nature, 1150–1750*, New York: Zone Books, 2001, p.16.

93
Aristotle, *Metaphysics* 1.2, 982b10–18, cited in *ibid.*, p.111.

94
Ibid., p.305.

95
Ibid., p.306.

96
Ibid., p.13.

97
Ibid., p.317.

98
Ibid., p.328.

99
Of course, such a brief overview necessarily contracts the historical shifts so closely examined by Daston and Park – their book is more than 500 pages long, including some 80 pages of endnotes and 50 of bibliography – and therefore ignores many more subtle movements and counter-movements within the period. Nevertheless, I hope that it provides even the slightest sense of a changing relationship between the two terms concerned, and facilitates their ongoing consideration in relation to the work of Fischli and Weiss.

100
One particular example cited by Daston and Park (p.109) is the *Quastiones naturals* of Adelard of Bath from the mid-twelfth century, a work that takes the form of 76 questions on the natural order posed to Adelard by his nephew. These include: Why do plants grow in places they have not been planted? Why don't human beings have horns? Why is the sea salty? Are the stars alive? These enquiries bring to mind Fischli and Weiss's work *Fragen*

(*Questions*), which has been presented in various forms from 1980 to 2003, most recently as slide projections, and was collected within the publication *Will Happiness Find Me?*, London: Alberta Press, n.d. The artists' questions include: Why does the earth turn a full circle once a day? Do souls wonder? Why do we stick to the ground? Is the world there when I am not?

101
L. Daston and K. Park, *Wonders and the Order of Nature, 1150–1750*, *op. cit.*, p.315.

102
In C. Bishop and M. Godfrey, 'Fischli and Weiss: Between Spectacular and Ordinary', *op. cit.*, p.76.

103
Martin Heidegger, 'What Calls for Thinking?', in David Farrell Krell (ed.), *Basic Writings*, London: Routledge, 1993, p.370.

104
Quoted in Brad Stone, 'Curiosity as the Thief of Wonder: An Essay on Heidegger's Critique of the Ordinary Conception of Time', *Kronoscope* 6.2, 2006, pp.205–29. A PDF of Stone's manuscript is available online at http://myweb.lmu.edu/bstone/writings.htm. The quotation is taken from p.5 of this version.

105
Ibid., p.6.

106
Ibid., p.7. There are others, however, who have argued that it might be worthwhile to reclaim a sense of curiosity, not least among them Michel Foucault:

Curiosity is a vice that has been stigmatised in turn by Christianity, by philosophy, and even by a certain conception of science. Curiosity, futility. The word, however, pleases me. To me it suggests something altogether different: it evokes 'concern'; it evokes the care one takes for what exists and could exist; a readiness to find strange and singular what surrounds us; a certain relentlessness to break up our familiarities and to regard otherwise the same things; a fervour to grasp what is happening and what passes; a casualness in regard to the traditional hierarchies of the important and the essential.

I dream of a new age of curiosity. We have the technical means for it; the desire is there; the things to be known are infinite; the people who can employ themselves at this task exist. Why do we suffer? From too little: from channels that are too narrow, skimpy, quasi-monopolistic, insufficient. There is no point in adopting a protectionist attitude, to prevent 'bad' information from invading and suffocating the 'good'. Rather, we must multiply the paths and the possibility of comings and goings.

Michel Foucault, 'The Masked Philosopher', in Sylvère Lotringer (ed.), *Foucault Live (Interviews, 1966–1984)* (trans. John Johnston), New York: Semiotext[e], 1989, pp.198–99. This is also quoted by L. Daston and K. Park, *Wonders and the Order of Nature, 1150–1750*, *op. cit.*, p.9.

107
B. Stone, 'Curiosity as the Thief of Wonder', *op. cit.*, p.9.

108
Ibid.

109
Tacita Dean, 'Send More Cups', in Bice Curiger, Peter Fischli and David Weiss (eds.), *Fischli Weiss – Flowers and Questions – A Retrospective*, London: Tate Publishing, 2006, p.109.